A GIFT FOR:

_____

FROM:

_____

THE BIBLE
ANSWER
BOOK

FROM THE BIBLE ANSWER MAN
HANK HANEGRAAFF

J COUNTRYMAN®

Nashville, Tennessee
www.jcountryman.com
A division of Thomas Nelson, Inc.
www.thomasnelson.com

www.thomasnelson.com
www.jcountryman.com

www.equip.org

Designed by UDG|DesignWorks, Sisters, Oregon

ISBN: 0–8499–9544–2

Printed and bound in Belgium

TO MY SON DAVID:

Your literary skills leave me speechless—
Your insights are profound

CONTENTS

INTRODUCTION

Larry King has had the opportunity to pose questions to more famous people than anyone else in history. Yet, if you listen carefully you'll discover that a handful of questions take precedence over all others. King once said that Jesus Christ was the person he would most like to interview—and the question he would most like to ask Christ is "Were you indeed born of a virgin?" According to King, the answer to this one question would define the rest of history.

Other questions King desperately wants answered are "Why do bad things happen to good people?" and "What makes the Bible more credible than the Qur'an?" During an interview on the Heaven's Gate cult suicides, he even asked me if Christianity itself could legitimately be considered a cult.

Like King, we too have pressing questions. Some want to know who created God, or what the purpose of prayer is if God already knows what we need before we ask him. Others want to know if it is ever morally permissible to lie, or if there is such a thing as ultimate truth. Still others want to know what happens to people who have never heard of Jesus Christ, or if the Bible promotes practices such as slavery.

For the last fifteen years, I have had the opportunity to answer thousands of such questions on a live nationally syndicated radio broadcast called the *Bible Answer Man*. Additionally, I've answered thousands more questions in venues around the world. In the process, I've gained a good grasp on the questions people most want answered—and these are precisely the ones I address in *The Bible Answer Book*.

I have taken my impromptu answers to questions and chiseled them until only the gem emerges. Moreover, as on my daily radio broadcast I not only suggest a recommended resource to stimulate further study, but I highlight a specific Scripture passage to fortify each question and answer.

Finally, a word about presentation. The reason I chose *J. Countryman* as the publisher for this project is that frankly no one but no one produces more beautiful books.

It is my prayer that *The Bible Answer Book* not only will equip you to "always be prepared to give an answer to everyone who asks you to give the reason for the hope that you have . . . with gentleness and respect" (1 Peter 3:15), but that it will be a treasure you share with family and friends.

HANK HANEGRAAFF
Rancho Santa Margarita, California

What Must I Do to Be Saved?

No one gets out of this world alive, so this is beyond a doubt the most important question you can ever ask yourself! In fact, the Bible was written, "so that you may know that you have eternal life" (1 John 5:13).

First, according to Scripture, you need to *realize* that you are a sinner. If you do not realize you are a sinner, you will not recognize your need for a savior. The Bible says we "all have sinned and fall short of the glory of God" (Romans 3:23).

Furthermore, you must *repent* of your sins. Repentance is an old English word that describes a willingness to turn from our sin towards Jesus Christ. It literally means a complete U-turn on the road of life—a change of heart and a change of mind. It means that you are willing to follow Jesus and to receive Him as your Savior and Lord. Jesus said, "repent and believe the Good News" (Mark 1:15).

Finally, to demonstrate true belief means to be willing to *receive*. To truly receive is to trust in and depend on Jesus Christ alone to be the Lord of our lives here and now and our Savior for all eternity. It takes more than *knowledge* (the devil knows about Jesus and trembles). It takes more than *agreement* that the knowledge we have is accurate (the devil agrees that Jesus is Lord). What it takes is to *trust* in Jesus Christ alone for eternal life. The requirements for eternal life are not based on what *you can do* but on what *Jesus Christ has done*. He stands ready to exchange his perfection for your imperfection.

The requirements for eternal life are not based on what you can do but on what Jesus Christ has done.

According to Jesus Christ, those who *realize* they are sinners, *repent* of their sins, and *receive* him as Savior and Lord are "born again" (John 3:3)—not physically, but spiritually. The reality of our salvation is not dependant on our feelings but rather on the promise of the Savior who says: "I tell you the truth, whoever hears my word and believes him who sent me has eternal life and will not be condemned; he has crossed over from death to life" (John 5:24).

See also Hank Hanegraaff, "Does your relationship with God make you sure you will go to heaven when you die?" pamphlet, available through Christian Research Institute, www.equip.org. For further study, see John MacArthur, *Hard to Believe: The High Cost and Infinite Value of Following Jesus* (Nashville: Thomas Nelson Publishers, 2003).

JOHN 3:16

"For God so loved the world that he gave his one and only Son, that whoever believes in him shall not perish but have eternal life."

If you confess with your mouth, "Jesus is Lord," and believe in your heart that God raised him from the dead, you will be saved. For it is with your heart that you believe and are justified, and it is with your mouth that you confess and are saved.

—ROMANS 10:9–10

WHAT ARE THE SECRETS
TO SPIRITUAL GROWTH?

ccording to Jesus Christ, those who repent and receive him as Savior and Lord are "born again" (John 3:3)—not physically, but spiritually. And with this spiritual birth must come spiritual growth. It is crucial therefore to be intimately acquainted with the ABCs of spiritual growth.

First, no relationship can flourish without constant, heartfelt communication. This is true not only in human relationships, but also in our relationship with God. If we are to nurture a strong relationship with our Savior, we must be in constant communication with him. The way to do that is through prayer.

Furthermore, it is crucial that we spend time reading God's written revelation of himself—the Bible. The Bible not only forms the foundation of an effective prayer life, but it is foundational to every other aspect of Christian living. While prayer is our primary way of communicating with God, the Bible is God's primary way of communicating with us.

Nothing should take precedence over getting into the Word and getting the Word into us. If we fail to eat well-balanced meals on a regular basis, we will eventually suffer the physical consequences. What is true of the outer man is also true of the inner man. If we do not regularly feed on the Word of God, we will starve spiritually.

Finally, it is crucial for new believers to become active participants in a healthy, well-balanced church. In Scripture, the church is referred to as the body of Christ. Just as our body is one and yet has many parts, so too the body of Christ is one but is composed of many members. Those who receive Christ as the Savior and Lord of their lives are already a part of the church universal. It is crucial, however, that all Christians become vital, reproducing members of a local body of believers as well.

For further study, see Hank Hanegraaff, *The Covering: God's Plan to Protect You from Evil* (Nashville: W Publishing Group, 2002).

HEBREWS 5:13–14
"Anyone who lives on milk, being still an infant,
is not acquainted with the teaching about
righteousness. But solid food is for the mature,
who by constant use have trained themselves
to distinguish good from evil."

– 3 –

WHAT IS SIN?

While it has become politically incorrect to talk about sin, the Scriptures make it crystal clear that "all have sinned and fall short of the glory of God" (Romans 3:23). But what is sin from a biblical perspective?

First, sin is not just murder, rape, or robbery. Sin is failing to do the things we should and doing those things that we should not. In short, *sin* is a word that describes anything that fails to meet God's standard of perfection. Thus, sin is the barrier between you and a satisfying relationship with God. Just as light and dark cannot exist together, neither can God and sin.

Furthermore, sin is a barrier between us and other people. You need only read the newspaper or listen to a news report to see how true this really is. We live in a time when terrorism abounds and when the world as we know it can be instantly obliterated by nuclear aggression.

Finally, sin is the deprivation of good. As such, sin is characterized by a lack of something rather than being something in itself. As noted above, sin is a break in relationship to God and others rather than being an ontological substance.

For further study, see Carl F. H. Henry, *Basic Christian Doctrines* (Grand Rapids: Baker Book House, 1962).

1 JOHN 3:4–6
"Everyone who sins breaks the law; in fact, sin is lawlessness. But you know that he appeared so that he might take away our sins. And in him is no sin. No one who lives in him keeps on sinning. No one who continues to sin has either seen him or known him."

SIN IS FAILING to do the things we should . . .

SINS OF OMISSION

Not forgiving (Matthew 6:15)

Failing to honor others
(Romans 12:9)

Failing to keep your fervor
(Romans, 12:9)

Failing to serve or give
(Romans, 12:9)

Failing to live at peace
(Romans 12:18)

Failing to love God
(Deuteronomy 6:4;
Mark 12:30)

Failing to love your neighbor
as yourself (Mark 12:31)

Failing to trust God
(Proverbs 3:5; Isaiah 26:4)

Failing to trust Christ
(John 14:1)

Failing to worship God
(Deuteronomy 6:13)

Failing to honor God
(Proverbs 3:9; John 5:23)

Failing to honor the Son
(John 5:23)

Failing to believe in Jesus
(John 3:16–18; 6:29)

Failing to honor one's
parents (Exodus 20:12)

Failing to give thanks to God
(Psalm 105:1; Romans 1:21)

Failing to glorify God (Psalm
34:3; Romans 1:21)

Failing to fear the Lord
(Deuteronomy 6:13;
Proverbs 3:7)

Failing to test new teaching by
Scripture (1 Thessalonians
5:21; Acts 17:11)

Failing to discern and guard
against false teachers and
prophets (Matthew
7:15–20; Acts 20:28–31)

Failing to learn and believe
Scripture (Deuteronomy
6:6; 2 Timothy 2:15)

Failing to guard life and
doctrine (1 Timothy 4:16)

Failing to repay debts
(Romans 13:7)

Failing to care for orphans
and widows in distress
(James 1:20)

Failing to defend the faith (1
Peter 3:15)

Failing to share the gospel
(Matthew 28:19)

and doing those things that we should not.

SINS OF COMMISSION

Wrong teaching
(Matthew 23:15)

Insincere love (Romans
12:9)

Causing someone else to sin
(Mark 9:42)

Sexual impurity (Romans
1:24)

Homosexuality
(Romans 1:26–27)

Idolatry (Romans 1:24)

Greed (Romans 1:29)

Blasphemy (Mark 3:29)

Misusing the Lord's name
(Exodus 20:7)

Selfish ambition
(Galatians 5:20)

Fits of rage (Galatians 5:20)

Slave trading (1 Timothy
1:10)

Lying (Exodus 23:1;
Revelation 21:8)

Hypocrisy (1 Peter 2:1)

Drunkenness
(1 Corinthians 6:10)

Stealing (Exodus 20:15;
1 Corinthians 6:10)

Sorcery (Deuteronomy
18:10)

Witchcraft
(Deuteronomy 18:10)

Divination
(Deuteronomy 18:10)

Interpreting Omens
(Deuteronomy 18:10)

Consulting the dead
(Deuteronomy 18:11)

Astrology (Deuteronomy
18:9–13; Isaiah 47:13–14)

Depravity (Romans 1:29)

Envy (Romans 1:29;
1 Peter 2:1)

Deceit (Romans 1:29;
1 Peter 2:1)

Murder (Romans 1:29)

Strife (Romans 1:29)

Malice (Romans 1:29;
1 Peter 2:1)

Gossip (Romans 1:29)

Slander (Romans 1:30;
1 Peter 2:1)

Hating God (Romans 1:30)

Insolence (Romans 1:30)

Arrogance (Romans 1:30)

Boastful (Romans 1:30)

Inventing evil (Romans 1:30)

Disobeying parents
(Romans 1:30)

— 4 —

How Can I Be Certain that I've Not Committed the Unforgivable Sin?

This is one of the most frequently asked questions on the *Bible Answer Man* broadcast and stems from the following words spoken by Christ: "I tell you the truth, every sin and blasphemy will be forgiven men, but the blasphemy against the Spirit will not be forgiven. Anyone who speaks a word against the Son of Man will be forgiven, but anyone who speaks against the Holy Spirit will not be forgiven, either in this age or in the age to come" (Matthew 12:31–32). As a result of these words, Christians are often paralyzed by fear.

In response, let me first point out that from a historic perspective the Pharisees mentioned by Matthew militantly hated Christ and attributed his miracles to Beelzebub, the prince of demons. Unlike those who are afraid they have committed the unforgivable sin, the Pharisees were totally unconcerned about Christ's forgiveness. Instead, with premeditation and persistence, they willfully blasphemed the Holy Spirit's testimony that Christ was the Son of the living God. It is crucial to recognize that the unforgivable sin is not a single act but a continuous, ongoing rejection.

Furthermore, those who have committed the unpardonable sin have no godly regrets. As Paul emphasizes in the book of Romans, they not only continue in their evil ways but approve of others who do so as well (Romans 1:32). Conversely, "godly sorrow brings repentance that leads to salvation" (2 Corinthians 7:10). Sorrow for sin and the desire for Christ's forgiveness is proof positive that you have not rejected the Savior of your soul. Never forget that three times Peter denied his Lord with vile oaths. Yet, Christ not only forgave him, but his confession, "You are the Christ, the Son of the living God" (Matthew 16:16) became the cornerstone of the Christian church.

Finally, the Bible consistently teaches that those who spend eternity separated from God do so because they willingly, knowingly, and continuously reject the gospel. John refers to this as the "sin that leads to death" (1 John 5:16) in the sense that those who refuse forgiveness through Christ will spend eternity separated from his grace and love. Be assured that those who sincerely desire God's forgiveness can be absolutely certain that they will never be turned away.

*The unforgivable sin
is not a single act but a continuous
ongoing rejection. . . . Those who
sincerely desire God's forgiveness can be
absolutely certain that they will
never be turned away.*

For further study see, Hank Hanegraaff, "The Unforgivable Sin," available from Christian Research Institute at http://www.equip.org.

To grow in your understanding of and relationship with God, see J. I. Packer, *Knowing God* (Downers Grove, Ill.: InterVarsity Press, 1993).

1 JOHN 5:13

"I write these things to you who believe in the name of the Son of God so that you may know that you have eternal life."

5

CAN A CHRISTIAN
LOSE THEIR SALVATION?

incere believers are sharply divided on this question. Some say Christians *can* lose their salvation and subsequently must be born again and again if they fall away. Others contend that true believers *cannot* lose their salvation through sin, but they can apostatize or walk away from their salvation. Still others hold that salvation begins at the moment of conversion (not death) and continues for all eternity—I hold this view for several reasons.

First, outward appearances can be deceiving. Consider Judas. For three years, he was part of Christ's inner circle. From all outward appearances, he was a true follower of Christ. Yet, Jesus characterized Judas as "a devil" (John 6:70). The book of Hebrews warns us that there were Jews who, like Judas, tasted God's goodness and yet turned from his grace. They acknowledged Christ with their lips, but their apostasy proved that their faith was not real.

Furthermore, we would do well to remember that everlasting life means just that—life everlasting. This life does not begin when we die but when we embrace the Savior who died in our place. As our physical birth can never be undone, so too our spiritual birth can never be undone. Christ said "Ye must be born again" (John 3:7, KJV), not "ye must be born again and again and again." In Philippians, Paul praises God for the confidence that, "He who began a good work in you will carry it on to completion" (Philippians 1:6).

Finally, Scripture is replete with passages that testify to the security of the believer. John 5:24 assures us that "he who believes . . . *has* eternal life"; 1 Corinthians 1:8 promises that Christ will "keep you strong to the end;" And Jude 24 guarantees that God "is able to keep you from falling and to present you before his glorious presence without fault." Moreover, Ephesians provides the surety that "you were marked in him with a seal, the promised Holy Spirit, who is a deposit guaranteeing our inheritance until the redemption of those who are God's possession" (1:13–14). As has been well said, the Lord's trees are evergreen.

For further study, see Hank Hanegraaff, "Safe and Secure," available from CRI at www.equip.org.

"*My sheep listen to my voice;*
I know them, and they follow me. I give them
eternal life, and they shall never perish; no one
can snatch them out of my hand.
My Father, who has given them to me,
is greater than all; no one can snatch them
out of my Father's hand."

6

WHAT IS THE BIBLICAL
DEFINITION OF FAITH?

he shield of faith described by the Apostle Paul in his letter to the Ephesian Christians is of paramount importance because it is the grace "with which you can extinguish all the flaming arrows of the evil one" (Ephesians 6:16). This is not an uncertain promise. Rather, it is divine assurance that faith equips us to escape the very extremities of evil. But what is faith?

First, the Bible defines faith as "being sure of what we hope for and certain of what we do not see" (Hebrews 11:1). Thus, in biblical vernacular, faith is a *channel of living trust*—an assurance—that stretches from man to God. In other words, it is the *object* of faith that renders faith faithful.

Furthermore, faith is the assurance that God's promises will never fail, even if sometimes we do not experience their fulfillment in our mortal existence. Hebrews 11 underscores the fact that we trust God to fulfill his promises for the future (the unseen) based on what he has already fulfilled in the past.

Thus, our faith is not blind, but based squarely on God's proven faithfulness.

Finally, the faith that serves to protect us in spiritual warfare is not to be confused with mere knowledge. Millions worldwide believe in the trustworthiness of Billy Graham. They have heard him proclaim the Good News on television and yet do not believe that his message corresponds to reality. Thus, they have the knowledge that it takes to be saved but do not have saving faith. Others hear the message, agree that it corresponds to reality, but due to the hardness of their hearts do not bow. Rather, like the demons, they continue to live in fearful anticipation of the judgment to come. (See James 2:19.) Some, however, have what Scripture describes as genuine justifying faith—a faith that not only knows about the gospel and agrees that its content corresponds to reality, but a faith by which they are transformed.

For further study, see Hank Hanegraaff, *The Covering: God's Plan to Protect You From Evil* (Nashville: W Publishing Group, 2002), chapter 7; and Hank Hanegraaff, *Christianity in Crisis* (Eugene, Ore.: Harvest House Publishers, 1993), Part 2.

JOB 13:15
"Though he slay me, yet will I hope in him."

— 7 —

What Does It Mean to Say
that the Holy Spirit Is in You?

Over the past several decades, I have been asked the "in" question in a variety of different ways such as: What does it mean to say God is "in" my life; Jesus is "in" my heart; or the Holy Spirit is "in" me? Does it mean that everyone simultaneously has a little piece of God in them? Or is the Bible communicating something far more precious?

First, to say that the Holy Spirit is *in* you is not to point out *where* the Holy Spirit is physically located, but rather to acknowledge that you have come into an intimate, personal relationship with him through faith and repentance. As such, the preposition "*in*" is not a *locational* but a *relational* term. Similarly, when Jesus says, "the Father is in me, and I in the Father" (John 10:38), He is not speaking of physical location but intimacy of relationship.

Furthermore, to deny that the Holy Spirit is *spatially* locatable within us is not to deny that he is *actively* locatable within us, working redemptively to conform us to the image of Christ. Far from detracting from our nearness to the Holy Spirit, the classical Christian view intensifies the intimacy of our relationship to the Creator as well as the benefits of our redemption.

Finally, according to the Scriptures, the Holy Spirit is not a physical being, thus to ask *where* the Holy Spirit is, is to confuse categories. Asking spatial questions about a Being who does not have extension in space makes about as much sense as asking what the color blue tastes like. King Solomon reveals the utter futility of believing that the infinite Holy Spirit can be physically contained in any finite space, let alone the human body, when he exclaimed, "Will God really dwell on earth? The heavens, even the highest heaven, cannot contain you. How much less this temple I have built!" (1 Kings 8:27).

For further study, see Hank Hanegraaff, "The Indwelling of the Holy Spirit," from CRI at www.equip.org.

1 CORINTHIANS 6:19
"Do you not know that your body is
a temple of the Holy Spirit, who is in you, whom you
have received from God?"

*If by the Spirit you put to death
the misdeeds of the body, you will live,
because those who are led
by the Spirit are sons of God.
For you did not receive a spirit that
makes you a slave again to fear,
but you received the Spirit of sonship.
And by him we cry, "Abba, Father."
The Spirit himself testifies with
our spirit that we are God's children.*

—ROMANS 8:13–16

8

How Were People Who Lived
before the Time of Christ Saved?

ome say that those who lived before the time of Christ were saved by keeping the law. The Scriptures, however, say otherwise.

First, the Bible from first to last demonstrates that the saved throughout history come to faith in exactly the same way—*by grace alone through faith alone on account of Christ alone.* The apostle Paul quotes the Old Testament extensively to drive home the reality that no one has been, or ever will be, declared righteous by observing the law (Romans 3:20).

Furthermore, Paul points to Abraham, the father of the Jews, to prove that salvation comes through faith apart from works that we perform. In his words, "If, in fact, Abraham was justified by works, he had something to boast about—but not before God. What does the Scripture say? 'Abraham believed God, and it was credited to him as righteousness'" (Romans 4:3; Genesis 15:6; Galatians 3:6–9).

Finally, Jesus Christ is the substance that fulfills the types and shadows in the Old Testament (Luke 24:44; Romans 3:21–22; Hebrews 1:1–3). Each year the Jews celebrated the Passover to keep them focused on the One who was to come to die for their sins (1 Corinthians 5:7; Hebrews 11:28, 39–40). As Hebrews says, "The law is only a shadow of the good things that are coming, not the realities themselves" (Hebrews 10:1).

The Bible from first to last demonstrates that the saved throughout history come to faith in exactly the same way—by grace alone through faith alone on account of Christ alone.

Jesus Christ stands at the apex of history. Just as people today look back in history to Christ's sacrifice on the cross, so too people who lived before the time of Christ looked forward to his sacrifice for them.

For further study see Bruce Milne, *Know the Truth* (Downer's Grove: InterVarsity Press: 1998), pages 189–191.

"What then shall we say that Abraham, our forefather,
discovered in this matter? If, in fact, Abraham was
justified by works, he had something to boast about—
but not before God. What does the Scripture say?
'Abraham believed God, and it was credited to him
as righteousness.' Now when a man works, his wages
are not credited to him as a gift, but as an obligation.
However, to the man who does not work but trusts
God who justifies the wicked, his faith is credited as
righteousness. David says the same thing when he
speaks of the blessedness of the man to whom God
credits righteousness apart from works: 'Blessed are they
whose transgressions are forgiven, whose sins are
covered. Blessed is the man whose sin the Lord will
never count against him.' Is this blessedness only for the
circumcised, or also for the uncircumcised? We have
been saying that Abraham's faith was credited to him
as righteousness. Under what circumstances was it
credited? Was it after he was circumcised,
or before? It was not after, but before!"

CAN A PERSON BE ARGUED
INTO THE KINGDOM OF GOD?

A common mistake Christians make derives from the notion that someone can be talked into the kingdom of God. While the motivation may be sincere, the consequences are often devastating.

First, no matter how eloquent you may or may not be, you cannot change anyone else's heart—only the Holy Spirit can do that. Thus while it is your responsibility to "always be prepared to give an answer to everyone who asks you to give the reason for the hope that you have" (1 Peter 3:15–16), it is God who changes the heart.

Furthermore, the problem is not that people *cannot* believe, it is that they *will not* believe. In other words, it is often not a matter of the mind but a matter of the will. To wit, the maxim: "A man convinced against his will is of the same opinion still." As Jesus Christ declared, "This is the verdict: Light has come into the world, but men loved darkness instead of light because their deeds were evil.

Everyone who does evil hates the light, and will not come into the light for fear that his deeds will be exposed" (John 3:19–20). The Christian faith is reasonable, but reason alone will not compel a person to embrace Christ.

Finally, I am utterly convinced that if we are "prepared to give an answer," God will bring into our paths those whose hearts he has prepared. Thus, it is our responsibility to prepare ourselves to be the most effective tools in the hands of Almighty God.

For further study, see William Lane Craig, *Reasonable Faith* (Crossway Books, 1994), chapter one.

1 Peter 3:15–16

*"But in your hearts set apart Christ as Lord.
Always be prepared to give an answer to everyone who
asks you to give the reason for the hope
that you have. But do this with gentleness and respect,
keeping a clear conscience, so that those
who speak maliciously against your good behavior in
Christ may be ashamed of their slander."*

How Do I Find a Good Church?

One of the questions I am most frequently asked is "How do I find a good church?" This question has taken on added significance in recent years because of the massive impact televangelism has had on our culture. In all too may cases, worship has been replaced with entertainment, and fellowship has been transformed into individualism. In view of these cultural developments, it is critical that Christians have a handle on the ingredients of a healthy well-balanced church.

The first sign of a healthy well-balanced church is a pastor who is committed to leading the community of faith in the *worship* of God through prayer, praise, and proclamation. *Prayer* is so inextricably woven into the fabric of worship that it would be unthinkable to have a church service without it. From the very inception of the early Christian church, prayer has been a primary means of worshiping God. Through prayer, we have the privilege of expressing adoration and thanksgiving to the One who saved us, sanctifies us, and one day will glorify us. In fact, our Lord himself set the pattern by teaching his disciples the Prayer of Jesus (Matthew 6:9-13).

Praise is another key ingredient of worship. Scripture urges us to "speak to one another with psalms, hymns and spiritual songs" (Ephesians 5:19). Singing psalms is a magnificent means for intercession, instruction, and the internalization of Scripture. In addition, the great hymns of the faith have stood the test of time and are rich in theological tradition and truth. Spiritual songs, in turn, communicate the freshness of our faith. Thus, it is crucial that we preserve both a respect for our spiritual heritage and a regard for contemporary compositions.

Along with prayer and praise, *proclamation* is axiomatic to experiencing vibrant worship. Paul urged his protégé Timothy to "preach the Word; be prepared in season and out of season; correct, rebuke and encourage—with great patience and careful instruction. For the time will come when men will not put up with sound doctrine. Instead, to suit their own desires, they will gather around them a great number of teachers to say what their itching ears want to hear" (2 Timothy 4:2–3). Church leaders must once again produce in their people a holy hunger for the Word of God. For it is through the proclamation of God's Word that believers are edified, exhorted, encouraged, and equipped.

Furthermore, a healthy well-balanced church is evidenced through its *oneness*. Christ breaks the barriers of gender, race, and background and unites us as one under the banner of his love. Such oneness is tangibly manifested through community, confession, and contribution.

Community is visible in baptism, which symbolizes our entrance into a body of believers who are one in Christ. It is a sign and a seal that we have been buried to our old life and raised to newness of life through his resurrection power. In like fashion, holy communion is an expression of oneness. As we all partake of the same elements, we partake of that which the elements symbolize— Christ, through whom we are one. Our fellowship on earth, celebrated through communion, is a foretaste of the heavenly fellowship we will share when symbol gives way to substance.

A further expression of our oneness in Christ is our common *confession* of faith—a core set of beliefs, which have been rightly referred to as "essential Christianity." These beliefs, which have been codified in the creeds of the Christian church, form the basis of our unity as the body of Christ. The well-known maxim bears repeating: "In essentials, unity; in nonessentials, liberty; and in all things, charity."

As with community and confession, we experience oneness through the *contribution* of our time, talent, and treasure. The question we should be asking is not "What can the church do for me?" but, "What can I do for the church?" The tragedy of modern Christianity is that when members of the body hurt, too often we relegate them to finding resources outside the walls of the church. That is precisely why the apostle Paul exhorts us to "share with God's people who are in need. Practice hospitality" (Romans 12:13).

Finally, a healthy well-balanced church is one that is committed to equipping believers to be effective *witnesses* to what they believe, why they believe, and Who they believe. In the Great Commission, Christ called believers not to make mere converts but to make disciples (Matthew 28:19). A disciple is a learner or follower of the Lord Jesus Christ. Thus, we must be prepared to communicate *what* we believe. In other words, we must be equipped to communicate the evangel. If Christians do not know how to share their faith, they have never been through basic training. The gospel of Christ should become such a part of our vocabulary that presenting it becomes second nature.

We also must be equipped to share *why* we believe what we believe. As Peter put it, we must "always be prepared to give an answer to everyone who asks you to give the *reason* for the hope that you have. But do this with gentleness and respect " (1 Peter 3:15). Too many today believe that the task of apologetics is the exclusive domain of scholars and theologians. Not so! The defense of the faith is not optional; it is basic training for *every Christian*.

In addition to being prepared to communicate the what and why of our faith, we must be empowered to communicate the *Who* of our faith. Virtually every theological heresy begins with a misconception of the nature of God. Thus, in a healthy well-balanced church believers are equipped to communicate glorious doctrines of the faith such as the Trinity and the deity of Jesus Christ. It is crucial that we, like the early Christian church, come to understand more fully the biblical concept of the priesthood of all believers. Clearly, it is not the pastor's calling to do the work of ministry single-handedly. Rather, the pastor is called "to prepare God's people for works of service, so that the body of Christ may be built up until we all reach unity in the faith and in the knowledge of the Son of God and become mature" (Ephesians 4:12–13).

In short, we know we have discovered a good church if God is *worshiped* in Spirit and in truth through prayer, praise and the proclamation of the Word; if the *oneness* we share in Christ is tangibly manifested through community, confession, and contribution; and if the church is equipping its members as *witnesses* who can communicate what they believe, why they believe, and Who they believe—WOW!

For further study see Hank Hanegraaff, "How to Find a Healthy Church," available from CRI at www.equip.org.

ACTS 2:42
"They [followers of Christ] devoted themselves
to the apostles' teaching and to the fellowship, to the
breaking of bread and to prayer."

We know we have discovered
a good church if . . .
God is worshiped in Spirit
and in truth through prayer,
praise and the proclamation of
the Word. The oneness
we share in Christ is tangibly
manifested through community,
confession, and contribution.
The church is equipping its
members as witnesses
who can communicate what
they believe, why they believe,
and Who they believe.

Let us not give up meeting

together as some are in the habit

of doing, but let us encourage one

another—and all the more

as you see the Day approaching.

—HEBREWS 10:25

WHY PRAY IF GOD
ALREADY KNOWS WHAT WE NEED?

A s the father of nine, I can tell you that I
sometimes know what my children need
before they ask. However, what I as an
earthly father only sometimes know, our eternal
Father always knows. Which inevitably leads to the
question: If God knows what we need before we
even ask, why bother asking at all?

First, it is crucial to recognize that supplication
should not be seen as the sole sum and substance of
prayers. Far from merely being a means of
presenting our daily requests to God, prayer is a
means of pursuing a dynamic relationship with him.

Furthermore, God ordains not only the ends
but the means. Thus, to ask, "Why pray if God
already knows what we need?" is akin to asking,
"Why get dressed in the morning and go to work?"
For that matter if God is going to do what he is
going to do anyway, why bother doing anything?
God has ordained that the work we do and the
prayers we utter both produce results. The fact that

God knows the future does not imply that our futures are fatalistically determined any more than our knowledge that the sun will rise causes the sun to rise.

Finally, while our Heavenly Father knows what we need before we even ask, our supplications are in and of themselves an acknowledgement of our dependence on him. And that alone is reason enough to pray without ceasing.

For further study, see Hank Hanegraaff, *The Prayer of Jesus: Secrets to Real Intimacy with God* (Nashville: W Publishing Group, 2001).

MATTHEW 6:7–8

"And when you pray, do not keep on babbling like pagans, for they think they will be heard because of their many words. Do not be like them, for your Father knows what you need before you ask him."

WHAT ARE SOME
SECRETS TO EFFECTIVE PRAYER?

Everyone wants to know the secret to something. Golfers want to know the secret to playing golf like Tiger Woods. Investors want to know the secret to making a fortune on Wall Street. Parents want to know the secret to raising healthy, happy kids. And Christians desperately want to know the secrets to effective prayer. So, what are the secrets to real intimacy with God?

The first secret to effective prayer is secret prayer. And Jesus provided the ultimate example. As Dr. Luke puts it, he "often withdrew to lonely places and prayed" (Luke 5:16). Unlike the religious leaders of his day, Jesus did not pray to be seen by men. He prayed because he treasured fellowship with his Father. Hypocrites gain their reward through public prayer. They may be perceived as spiritual giants, but by the time they are finished, they have received everything they will ever get—their prayer's worth and nothing more.

A further secret is to recognize the connection between prayer and meditation. Our prayers are only as inspired as our intake of Scripture. Scripture feeds meditation, and meditation gives food to our prayers. Meditating on Scripture allows us to more naturally transition into a marvelous time of meaningful prayer. Donald Whitney, who rightly refers to meditation as the missing link between the intake of Scripture and prayer, notes that if there was a secret to the prayer life of evangelist George Müller, it was his discovery of the connection between meditation and prayer.

A final secret is to discover your secret place, a place where you can drown out the static of the world and hear the voice of your heavenly Father. The issue, of course, is not location but motivation. We are all unique creations of God. Thus, your secret place will no doubt be different than mine. The point is that we all desperately need a place away from the invasive sounds of this world so that we can hear the sounds of another place and another Voice.

For further study see, Hank Hanegraaff, *The Prayer of Jesus: Secrets to Intimacy with God* (Nashville: W Publishing Group, 2001).

*"But when you pray, go into your room,
close the door and pray to your Father, who is unseen.
Then your Father, who sees what is done
in secret, will reward you."*

A FEW PRAYERS IN THE BIBLE:

Abraham's servant—Genesis 24:12–14—Prayed
  for success in finding a wife for Isaac

Jacob—Genesis 32:9–12—Prayed for protection

Job—Job 13:23—Prayed for conviction of sin

Moses—Exodus 32:11–13, 31–32; Deuteronomy
  9:26–29—Prayed for mercy

Moses—Exodus 33:12–18—Prayed to know God
  and to see his glory

Manoah—Judges 13:8—Prayed for guidance in
  raising his son, Samson

Hannah—1 Samuel 2:1–10—Prayed to exalt
  God with thanksgiving and praise

Elijah—1 Kings 18:36–37—Prayed for
  vindication and proof of God's power

Hezekiah—2 Kings 19:15–19—Prayed for
  deliverance from enemies

Solomon—2 Chronicles 6:21—Prayed for
  forgiveness of sins for Israel

David—throughout Psalms—Prayed with
  thanksgiving and praise for mercy and
  grace, conviction of sin, forgiveness,
  instruction, and deliverance from enemies

Jeremiah—Jeremiah 20:7–18—Prayed to complain

Ezra—Ezra 9:6–15—Prayed to confess his people's sin

Daniel—Daniel 6:10-11—Prayed for help with thanksgiving

Daniel—Daniel 9:9–19—Prayed to confess his people's sin

Jonah—Jonah 2:1–9—Prayed for restoration

Jesus—Matthew 26:36–46—Prayed for God's will

Jesus—John 17—1–26—Prayed for himself, for the disciples, and for all believers

Jesus—Luke 23:34—Prayed for forgiveness for his enemies

Apostles—Acts 1:24–25—Prayed for selecting Judas' replacement

Apostles—Acts 4:29---30—Prayed for the bold proclamation of the gospel with miracles

Stephen—Acts 7:59-60—Prayed for the Lord to receive his spirit and to forgive his killers

WHY IS IT SO CRUCIAL TO PRAY
'YOUR WILL BE DONE?'

esus not only taught his disciples to pray, "Your will be done" (Matthew 6:10), but he modeled those very words in his own life and ministry. Which of course begs the question, "Why is it so crucial to pray in this way?"

First, to pray "your will be done" is to recognize the sovereignty of God over every aspect of our daily lives. In effect, it is a way of saying, "Thank God this world is under his control, not mine!" We would be in deep trouble if God gave us everything for which we asked. Fact is, we don't know what's best for us! We only see a snapshot of our lives—while God sees the entire panoply. Thus, his perspective is far superior to ours.

Furthermore, to pray "your will be done" is daily recognition that our wills must be submitted to his will. One of the most comforting thoughts that can penetrate a human mind yielded to the will of God is that he who has created us also knows what is best for us. Thus, if we walk according to his will, rather than trying to command him according to our own wills, we will indeed have, as he promised, not a panacea, but peace in the midst of the storm. In the yielded life there is great peace in knowing that the One who taught us to pray "your will be done" has every detail of our lives under control. Not only is God the object of our faith, he is also the originator of our faith. Indeed, he is the originator of our salvation and, yes, even the originator of our prayers. Thus, whatever we pray for, whether it's healing or a house, when our will is in harmony with his will, we will receive what we request one hundred percent of the time. However, when we pray as Christ prayed, "Nevertheless, not my will but thy will be done," we can rest assured that even in sickness and tragedy "all things work together for good to those who love God and are called according to his purpose" (Romans 8:28).

Finally, to pray "your will be done" is daily recognition that God will not spare us from trial and tribulation, but rather he will use the fiery furnace to purge impurities from our lives. Ultimately, this is the message of the book of Job. Job endured more tragedy in a single day than most people experience in a lifetime. Yet in his darkest hour Job uttered the ultimate words of faith, "Though He slay me, yet will I trust in Him" (Job 13:15, KJV). For the child of God the hope is not perfect health and happiness in this lifetime, but a resurrected body and a heavenly dwelling in the life to come.

For further study, see Hank Hanegraaff, *The Prayer of Jesus: Secrets to Real Intimacy with God* (Nashville: W Publishing Group, 2001).

JAMES 4:13–16

"Now listen, you who say, 'Today or tomorrow we will go to this or that city, spend a year there, carry on business and make money.' Why, you do not even know what will happen tomorrow. What is your life? You are a mist that appears for a little while and then vanishes. Instead, you ought to say, 'If it is the Lord's will, we will live and do this or that.' As it is, you boast and brag. All such boasting is evil."

To pray "your will be done" is daily recognition that God will not spare us from trial and tribulation, but rather he will use the fiery furnace to purge impurities from our lives.

14

WHY DO PEOPLE END THEIR
PRAYERS WITH THE WORD 'AMEN'?

∽

Everyone is familiar with the word "amen." But have you ever taken the time to consider what it really means? Is ending our prayers with "amen" a mere ritual? Or is there a majestic richness to the word that is often missed?

First, "amen" is a universally recognized word that is far more significant than simply signing off or saying, "That's all." With the word "amen" we are in effect saying, "May it be so in accordance with the will of God." It is a marvelous reminder that any discussion on prayer must begin with the understanding that prayer is a means of bringing us into conformity with God's will, not a magic mantra that ensures God's conformity to ours.

Furthermore, the word "amen" is a direct reference to Jesus, who taught us to pray "your will be done" (Matthew 6:10). In Revelation, he is referred to as the "Amen, the faithful and true witness, the ruler of God's creation" (Revelation 3:14). Jesus not only taught us to pray, "your will be done," he modeled those words in his life. In his passionate prayer in the Garden of Gethsemane he prayed, "My Father, if it is possible, may this cup be taken from me. Yet *not as I will, but as you will*" (Matthew 26:39, emphasis added).

Finally, although Jesus is our greatest example, he is certainly not our only example. His brother James warns those who are prone to "boast and brag" that they ought to pray instead, "If it is the Lord's will, we will live and do this or that" (James 4:15). Christ's closest friend during His earthly ministry, the apostle John, echoes the words of the Master when he writes, "This is the confidence we have in approaching God: that if we ask anything *according to his will*, he hears us" (1 John 5:14, emphasis added).

Next time you end your prayer time with the word "amen" it is my prayer that you will focus on the fact that far from being a formality, it is fraught with meaning. Not only is "amen" a direct reference to the Savior, but it is a reminder that even the seemingly insignificant details of our lives are under the Savior's sovereign control.

For further study, see Hank Hanegraaff, *The Prayer of Jesus: Secrets to Real Intimacy with God* (Nashville: W Publishing Group, 2001).

"This is the confidence we have in approaching God: that if we ask anything according to his will, he hears us. And if we know that he hears us—whatever we ask—we know that we have what we asked of him."

*Prayer is a means
of bringing us into conformity
with God's will, not a magic
mantra that ensures God's
conformity to ours.*

DOES ISAIAH 53:5
GUARANTEE OUR HEALING TODAY?

he mantra "by his stripes we are healed" is repeated endlessly in Christian circles. However, these words extracted from Isaiah 53:5 focus on *spiritual* rather than *physical* healing.

First, a quick look at the context makes it clear that Isaiah had *spiritual* rather than *physical* healing in mind: Christ "was wounded for our *transgressions*, He was bruised for our *iniquities*; The chastisement for our peace was upon Him, And by His stripes we are healed" (Isaiah 53:5, NKJV, emphasis added). Peter builds on this understanding when he writes, "He himself bore our *sins* in his body on the tree, so that we might die to *sins* and live for righteousness; by his wounds you have been healed" (1 Peter 2:24).

Furthermore, while healing for the body is not referred to in Isaiah 53:5, it is referred to in the verse *immediately* preceding it. Here Isaiah writes, "Surely he has borne our griefs and carried our sorrows; Yet we esteemed Him stricken, smitten by God, and afflicted" (Isaiah 53:4, NKJV). *Physical* healing here is not only clear in context, but is affirmed by the Gospels where it is given an important qualification: "When evening came, many who were demon-possessed were brought to him, and he drove out the spirits with a word and healed all the sick. This was to fulfill what was spoken through the prophet Isaiah: 'He took up our infirmities and carried our diseases'" (Matthew 8:16–17). Thus, the healing here was *fulfilled* during the ministry of Christ and does not *guarantee* healing today.

Finally, I should note that in a real sense Christ's atonement on the cross *does* extend to *physical* healing. One day, "there will be no more death or mourning or crying or pain, for the old order of things has passed away" (Revelation 21:4). However, as Paul points out, "We hope for *what we do not yet have*, we *wait* for it patiently" (Romans 8:25, emphasis added). In the meantime, we will all experience sickness and suffering. Indeed, those who live before Christ returns will all die of their last disease—the death rate is one per person and we're all going to make it!

For further study, see Hank Hanegraaff, *Christianity in Crisis* (Eugene, Ore.: Harvest House Publishers, 1993).

"Surely he took up our infirmities
and carried our sorrows,
yet we considered him stricken by God,
smitten by him, and afflicted.
But he was pierced for our transgressions,
he was crushed for our iniquities;
the punishment that brought us peace was upon him,
and by his wounds we are healed.
We all, like sheep, have gone astray,
each of us has turned to his own way;
and the LORD has laid on him
the iniquity of us all."

16

MUST I FORGIVE THOSE
WHO REFUSE FORGIVENESS?

esus taught his disciples to pray, "Forgive us our debts, as we also have forgiven our debtors" (Matthew 6:12). Does that mean we have to forgive someone even when they refuse reconciliation?

First, the debts we owe one another are small change compared to the infinite debt we owe our heavenly Father. Because we have been forgiven an infinite debt, it is a horrendous evil to even consider withholding forgiveness from those who seek it. Thus, we must always manifest the kind of love that is *willing* to forgive those who wrong us.

Furthermore, forgiveness is by definition a two-way street leading to the restoration of fellowship. It requires someone who is *willing* to forgive, and someone who is *wanting* to be forgiven. If you are to forgive me, I must be repentant; otherwise, there can be no restoration of fellowship (i.e. forgiveness).

Finally, we must never suppose that our standard of forgiveness is higher than God's standard. He *objectively* offers us forgiveness and the restoration of fellowship. His forgiveness is not *subjectively* realized, however, until we repent (Luke 6:37–38).

For further study, see Hank Hanegraaff, *The Prayer of Jesus: Secrets to Real Intimacy with God* (Nashville: W. Publishing Group, 2001).

MATTHEW 5:23–24

"Therefore, if you are offering your gift at the altar and there remember that your brother has something against you, leave your gift there in front of the altar. First go and be reconciled to your brother; then come and offer your gift."

THE IMPORTANCE OF FORGIVENESS is underscored in one of the most riveting parables Jesus ever communicated to his disciples. It was the story of two debtors. The first owed his master an amount comparable to twenty million dollars—more than he could pay if he lived to be a thousand years old. The second debtor owed the first debtor less than twenty dollars. When the day of reckoning came, the master forgave the multi-million-dollar debtor every last penny. Instead of being overwhelmed with gratitude, however, the man who was forgiven much tracked down the man who owed him little, grabbed him by the throat, and dragged him away to debtors' prison. When the master heard all that had happened, his condemnation was swift and severe. The ungrateful servant was thrown into jail to be tortured until he could repay his debt in full.

When Jesus finished telling the story, he turned to his disciples and said, "This is how my heavenly Father will treat each of you unless you forgive your brother from your heart" (Matthew 18:35). The disciples immediately got the point. The debts we owe one another are like mere twenty-dollar bills compared to the infinite debt we owe our heavenly Father. Because we have been forgiven an infinite debt, it is a horrendous evil to even consider withholding forgiveness from those who seek it. If, even for a moment, we might wonder whether or not to forgive our debtors, this parable immediately should soften our hearts and illumine the darkness of our minds.

MATTHEW 18:23–35, NKJV

"The kingdom of heaven is like a certain king who wanted to settle accounts with his servants. And when he had begun to settle accounts, one was brought to him who owed him ten thousand talents. But as he was not able to pay, his master commanded that he be sold, with his wife and children and all that he had, and that payment be made. The servant therefore fell down before him, saying, 'Master, have patience with me, and I will pay you all.' Then the master of that servant was moved with compassion, released him, and forgave him the debt.

"But that servant went out and found one of his fellow servants who owed him a hundred denarii; and he laid hands on him and took him by the throat, saying, 'Pay me what you owe!' So his fellow servant fell down at his feet and begged him, saying, 'Have patience with me, and I will pay you all.' And he would not, but went and threw him into prison till he should pay the debt. So when his fellow servants saw what had been done, they were very grieved, and came and told their master all that had been done. Then his master, after he had called him, said to him, 'You wicked servant! I forgave you all that debt because you begged me. Should you not also have had compassion on your fellow servant, just as I had pity on you?' And his master was angry, and delivered him to the torturers until he should pay all that was due to him.

"So My heavenly Father also will do to you if each of you, from his heart, does not forgive his brother his trespasses."

17

Why Do Christians Worship on Sunday Rather than on the Sabbath Day?

Although some Christian traditions denounce Sunday worship as the end time "mark of the beast," there are good reasons why millions of Christians gather on the first day of the week for worship.

First, in remembrance of the resurrection the early Christian church changed the day of worship from Saturday to Sunday. Within weeks, thousands of Jews willingly gave up a theological tradition that had given them their national identity. God himself had provided the early church with a new pattern of worship through Christ's resurrection on the first day of the week as well as the Holy Spirit's descent on Pentecost Sunday.

Furthermore, Scripture provides us with the reasons behind the symbol of the Sabbath. In Genesis, the Sabbath was a celebration of God's work in creation (Genesis 2:2–3; Exodus 20:11). After the Exodus, the Sabbath expanded to a celebration of God's deliverance from oppression in

Egypt (Deuteronomy 5:15). As a result of the resurrection, the Sabbath's emphasis shifted once again. It became a celebration of the "rest" we have through Christ who delivers us from sin and the grave (Hebrews 4:1–11). For the emerging Christian church, the most dangerous snare was a failure to recognize that Jesus was the substance that fulfilled the symbol of the Sabbath.

In the end, religious rites must
inevitably bow to redemptive realities.

Finally, if you insist on being slavishly bound to Old Testament laws you should also be forewarned that failing to keep the letter of the law might be hazardous to your health. According to the Mosaic Law, anyone who does any work on the Sabbath "must be put to death" (Exodus 35:2). As the apostle Paul explains, however, "Christ redeemed us from the curse of the law by becoming a curse for us, for it is written: 'Cursed is everyone who is hung on a tree'"(Galatians 3:13). The Sabbath was "a shadow of the things that were to come; the reality, however, is found in Christ" (Colossians

2:17). In the end, religious rites must inevitably bow to redemptive realities.

For further study, see D.A. Carson, ed., *From Sabbath to Lord's Day: A Biblical, Historical, and Theological Investigation* (Eugene, Oregon: Wipf and Stock Publishers, 1999, originally published by Zondervan, 1982)

COLOSSIANS 2:16–17

"Do not let anyone judge you by what you eat or drink, or with regard to a religious festival, a New Moon celebration or a Sabbath day. These are a shadow of the things that were to come; the reality, however, is found in Christ."

On the first day of the week, very early in the morning, the women took the spices they had prepared and went to the tomb. They found the stone rolled away from the tomb, but when they entered, they did not find the body of the Lord Jesus. While they were wondering about this, suddenly two men in clothes that gleamed like lightning stood beside them. In their fright the women bowed down with their faces to the ground, but the men said to them, "Why do you look for the living among the dead? He is not here; he has risen!"

—LUKE 24:1–6

18

IS THE TITHE FOR TODAY?

f all the questions I am asked to answer, this is beyond a doubt the most difficult. Not only because the subject of tithing is hotly debated, but because I must confess that I personally have not always been faithful in giving a tenth or more to the work of the Lord. And I am not alone. Research demonstrates that the vast majority of Christians not only do not tithe regularly, but many give little or nothing at all. Thus, while addressing this question is incredibly convicting, it also is increasingly crucial.

First, as Randy Alcorn has well said, tithing may well be regarded as the training wheels of giving. As such, tithing is as important today as it has ever been. We all need to learn what it is to stride free and unfettered down the path of Christian stewardship. For in learning to give we also are learning to lean more heavily upon our heavenly Father and less heavily upon ourselves. Those who have traveled the Calvary road for any length of time surely can testify to the truth that God is ever faithful. Not only so, but as we weekly set aside our tithes and offerings we are reminded that all we are, or ever hope to be, is a gift from God.

Furthermore, as Moses communicated to the children of Israel, we tithe "so that [we] may learn to revere the Lord [our] God always" (Deuteronomy 14:23). As we all know, learning to reverence the name of God is a timeless principle—as crucial today as in the days of Moses. Long *before* Moses, the Bible records Jacob's promise to God: "Of all that you give me I will give you a tenth" (Genesis 28:22). Long *after* Moses, Jesus reaffirmed the practice of tithing (Matthew 23:23)—not for outward appearances but as an outward expression of an inward reality. Additionally, in the fourth century the great church father Jerome echoed the words of Malachi who intimated that failing to pay tithes and offerings was tantamount to "robbing" God—a prescription for financial ruin (Malachi 3:8).

Finally, it should be noted that tithing in the Old Testament not only prepared God's people to become hilarious givers but produced a temple of unparalleled splendor. The Israelites who pined for the pleasures and protection of pagan Egypt more than for the One who had miraculously parted the Red Sea had been transformed into joyful givers.

The Bible chronicles the prayer of David as he thanked God for the very privilege of being able to give to the work of the Lord: "But who am I, and who are my people, that we should be able to give as generously as this? Everything comes from you, and we have given you only what comes from your hand . . . and now I have seen with joy how willingly your people who are here have given to you" (1 Chronicles 29:14, 17).

What began as a spiritual discipline had evolved into sheer delight.

There is no telling what can be accomplished in our generation if we, too, may but catch the joy of contagious giving. Not only would we be empowered to spread the gospel around the globe, but we would be enabled to feed the hungry, clothe the naked, and care for the sick. Like our forefathers who founded great centers of Christian education, established countless hospitals, and funded myriad relief organizations we might yet leave an indelible mark on our generation. For only when the training wheels of tithing come off will the world of free will giving become our playground.

There is no telling what
can be accomplished in our generation
if we, too, may but catch the joy
of contagious giving.

For further study, see Randy Alcorn, *Money, Possessions and Eternity*, rev. ed. (Wheaton, Ill.: Tyndale House Publishers, 2003).

PROVERBS 3: 9–10

"Honor the LORD with your wealth, with the firstfruits of all your crops;
then your barns will be filled to overflowing, and your vats will brim over with new wine."

My Budget

God's Money   100%

Tithing   10%

Taking care of the
family and neighbors
entrusted to me by God   70%

Saving for times of need and
special opportunities
to serve   20%

19

WHAT IS THE BIBLICAL VIEW OF WEALTH?

I am persuaded that the Bible teaches a form of Christian capitalism—in other words, responsibility associated with wealth. It does not promote the possession of money for the sake of money, but instead encourages us to use money for the sake of the kingdom. In short, a biblical view of wealth involves an eternal perspective.

First, it is crucial to realize that "The earth is the LORD's and everything in it, the world, and all who live in it" (Psalm 24:1). God is the Landlord; we are just tenants. We did not arrive with anything, and we will not take anything with us when we leave. Just remembering this fact of life will save us from a world of hurt.

Furthermore, poverty does not equal piety; nor do riches equal righteousness. God prospers some, and he puts others in more humble circumstances. If there were a one-to-one ratio between godliness and wealth, the godliest people in the world would be the wealthiest. A quick check of the Forbes 500 will quickly dash such an illusion.

Finally, it is important to view wealth with eternity in mind. In other words, lead your life here below as a responsible steward—whether you have a little or a lot—so that one day, at the judgment, God himself will richly reward you (Matthew 25:21). It is your bank statement in *heaven* that counts (Matthew 6:19–21); if you fix your hope on the one you have down here, you are bankrupt no matter how many digits you count next to your name.

For further study, see John Piper, *Desiring God: Meditations of a Christian Hedonist* (Sisters, Ore.: Multnomah Publishers, 1986), chapter 7. Also see Hank Hanegraaff, *Christianity in Crisis* (Eugene, Ore.: Harvest House Publishers, 1993), Part 5.

MATTHEW 6:24
"No one can serve two masters.
Either he will hate the one and love the other,
or he will be devoted to the one and despise the other.
You cannot serve both God and Money."

*A biblical view
of wealth involves an
eternal perspective.*

20

Is Being 'Slain in the Spirit' Consistent with a Biblical Worldview?

Today thousands of people are routinely being "slain in the spirit" in the name of a fashionable and palpable demonstration of Holy Ghost power. Practitioners claim ample validation for this phenomenon in Scripture, church history, and experience. However, the phenomenon is not only conspicuous by its absence in the ministry of Jesus and the Apostles, but is generally inconsistent with a biblical worldview.

First, as aptly noted by pro-Pentecostal sources such as the *Dictionary of Pentecostal and Charismatic Movements (DPCM)* (Grand Rapids: Zondervan, 1988), "An entire battalion of Scripture proof texts is enlisted to support the legitimacy of the phenomenon, although Scripture plainly offers no support for the phenomenon as something to be expected in the normal Christian life" (p.790).

Furthermore, the experience of being "slain in the spirit" can be attributed to mere human manipulation. According to the *DPCM*, "in addition to God, the source of the experience can be a purely human response to autosuggestion, group 'peer pressure,' or simply a desire to experience the phenomenon" (p.789). Cynics may write off the use of altered states of consciousness, peer pressure, expectations, and suggestive powers as mere socio-psychological manipulation, but Christians must perceive an even more significant threat—these techniques are fertile soil for satanic and spiritual deception.

Finally, the "slain in the spirit" phenomenon has more in common with occultism than with a biblical worldview. As popular "slain in the spirit" practitioner Francis MacNutt candidly confesses in his book *Overcome by the Spirit*, the phenomenon is externally similar to "manifestations of voodoo and other magic rites" and is "found today among different sects in the Orient as well as among primitive tribes of Africa and Latin America." In sharp contrast, Scripture makes it clear that as Christians we must be "self-controlled and alert" (1 Peter 5:8) rather than being in an altered state of consciousness or "slain in the spirit."

"Slain in the spirit"
is a fashionable description
for a person falling
backwards due to a supposed
encounter with the
power of the Holy Spirit.

For further study, see Hank Hanegraaff, *Counterfeit Revival: Looking for God in All the Wrong Places*, rev. ed. (Nashville: Word Publishing, 2001).

1 PETER 5:8–9

"Be self-controlled and alert. Your enemy the devil prowls around like a roaring lion looking for someone to devour. Resist him, standing firm in the faith."

SHOULD CHRISTIANS
CELEBRATE CHRISTMAS?

very year around Christmas time, serious concerns are voiced regarding the validity of celebrating Christmas. Some note that the origins of Christmas are pagan, others point out that the Bible overtly denounces Christmas trees as idolatrous, and still others suggest that Santa Claus is a dangerous fairy tale.

In response let me first acknowledge that when Christmas was originally instituted, December 25th was indeed a pagan festival commemorating the birthday of a false god. While this is historical fact, what is frequently overlooked is that the church's choice of December 25th was intentional. Instead of Christianizing a pagan festival, the church established a rival celebration. While the world has all but forgotten the Greco-Roman gods of antiquity, they are annually reminded that two thousand years ago Christ invaded time and space.

Furthermore, the Bible nowhere condemns Christmas trees as idolatrous. The oft-cited passage in Jeremiah 10:2–4 might at first blush appear compelling, but context precludes the pretext. Jeremiah's description of a tree cut out of the forest adorned with silver and gold and fastened with a hammer and nails so that it would not totter is a reference to wooden idols, not Christmas trees. In fact, Christmas trees originated in Christian Germany two thousand years after Jeremiah's condemnation of manmade idols. They evolved over time from two Christian traditions. One was a "paradise tree" hung with apples as a reminder of the tree of life in the Garden of Eden. The other was a triangular shelf holding Christmas figurines decorated by a star. In the sixteenth century, these two symbols merged into the present Christmas tree tradition. Next Christmas you might well consider using the Christmas tree in the home of an unbeliever as a springboard or opportunity to explain the reason for the season from the fall in Paradise to redemption in Christ.

Finally, believe it or not, even Santa can be saved! Far from merely being a dangerous fairy tale, "Santa Claus" in reality is an Anglicized form of the Dutch name *Sinter Klaas,* which in turn is a reference to Saint Nicholas. According to tradition, Saint Nick not only lavished gifts on needy children but also valiantly supported the doctrine of the Trinity at the Council of Nicea in 325 A.D. Thus, Christians may legitimately look to Saint Nick as a genuine hero of the faith.

This December 25th as you celebrate the coming of Christ with a Christmas tree surrounded by presents, may the selflessness of Saint Nick be a reminder of the Savior who gave the greatest gift of all: "Greater love has no one than this, that he lay down his life for his friends" (John 15:13).

For further study, see Paul Maier, *The First Christmas* (Grand Rapids: Kregel Publications, 2001).

Luke 2:8–14

"And there were shepherds living out in the fields nearby, keeping watch over their flocks at night. An angel of the Lord appeared to them, and the glory of the Lord shone around them, and they were terrified. But the angel said to them, 'Do not be afraid. I bring you good news of great joy that will be for all the people. Today in the town of David a Savior has been born to you; he is Christ the Lord. This will be a sign to you: You will find a baby wrapped in cloths and lying in a manger.' Suddenly a great company of the heavenly host appeared with the angel, praising God and saying, 'Glory to God in the highest, and on earth peace to men on whom his favor rests.'"

HOW SHOULD CHRISTIANS
RESPOND TO HALLOWEEN?

yriad questions surround Halloween.
Should we participate? Accommodate?
Or should we vigorously denounce
Halloween? To answer such questions, it's helpful
to view Halloween from the perspective of history.

First, we should recognize that Halloween is
indeed rooted in the ancient Celtic feast of *Samhain*
(sah-ween). The Druids believed that on the eve of
Samhain the veil between the present world and the
world beyond was pierced, releasing demons, witches,
and hobgoblins en masse to harass the living. In order
to make themselves immune from attack, people
disguised themselves as witches, devils, and ghouls;
attempted to ward off evil spirits by carving grotesque
faces on gourds illuminated with candles; and
placated the spirits with a variety of treats.

Furthermore, we can learn a lot from how the
early Christians responded to Halloween. October
31st, the eve prior to All Saints Day was designated
as a spiritually edifying holiday (holy day) on which

*The trick is to treat
Halloween as a
strategic opportunity rather than a
time of satanic oppression.*

to proclaim the supremacy of the gospel over the superstition of ghosts. Thus, "all Hallows Eve," from which the word Halloween is derived, was an attempt on the part of Christianity to overwhelm the tradition of ghouls with the truth of the Gospel.

Finally, although Halloween is once again predominately pagan there is a silver lining. Like our forefathers, we can choose to celebrate "all Hallows Eve" by focusing on heroes of the faith—those who, like Martin Luther, were willing to stand for truth no matter what the cost. We might also use the occasion to introduce our children to such great classics as *Pilgrim's Progress*. In the end, the trick is to treat Halloween as a strategic opportunity rather than a time of satanic oppression.

See also Hank Hanegraaff, "Halloween: Oppression or Opportunity?" Available from CRI, www.equip.org.

HEBREWS 12:1

"Therefore, since we are surrounded by such a great cloud of witnesses, let us throw off everything that hinders and the sin that so easily entangles, and let us run with perseverance the race marked out for us."

Is the 'Binding and Loosing'
of Demons Biblical?

ne of the most common expressions in contemporary Christianity is "I bind you, Satan, in the name of Jesus." Biblically however, the phrase "binding and loosing" has nothing whatsoever to do with demons.

First, when Jesus told the disciples, "whatever you bind on earth will be bound in heaven, and whatever you loose on earth will be loosed in heaven" (Matthew 16:19) he was not talking about demons but discipline. In other words, in the context of church discipline, those who repent are to be "loosed" (i.e. restored to fellowship). Those who persist in sin are to be "bound" (i.e. removed from fellowship). Demons are totally foreign to the context.

Furthermore, humans are not authorized anywhere in Scripture to "bind or loose" Satan. Even the archangel Michael did not tackle Satan on his own. Despite his wisdom and power, he called on God to rebuke Satan. Christians should never suppose that they are smart enough to engage Satan on their own. Rather they, like Michael, should pray, "The Lord rebuke you" (Jude 9).

Finally, while it makes sense to ask the Lord to "bind" the power of demons in the sense of thwarting their plans to undo us, to "loose" Satan and his minions makes no sense at all. Thus, common sense alone should be enough to convince us that biblically "binding and loosing" has nothing whatsoever to do with demons.

For further study on biblical spiritual warfare, see Hank Hanegraaff, *The Covering: God's Plan to Protect You from Evil* (Nashville: W Publishing, 2002).

MATTHEW 18:15–20

"If your brother sins against you, go and show him his fault, just between the two of you. If he listens to you, you have won your brother over. But if he will not listen, take one or two others along, so that 'every matter may be established by the testimony of two or three witnesses.' If he refuses to listen to them, tell it to the church; and if he refuses to listen even to the church, treat him as you would a pagan or a tax collector.
"I tell you the truth, whatever you bind on earth will be bound in heaven, and whatever you loose on earth will be loosed in heaven.

*"Again, I tell you that if two of you
on earth agree about anything you ask for,
it will be done for you by my Father in heaven.
For where two or three come
together in my name, there am I with them."*

CAN CHRISTIANS BE DEMONIZED?

ver the years, I have read a wide variety of stories that claim to support the notion that Christians can be demonized. In the end, they all have one thing in common: They greatly overestimate the power and province of Satan. Some deliverance ministers make a more valiant attempt than others to provide a biblical basis for the contention that a Christian can be inhabited by a demon. Inevitably, however, Scripture itself undermines their stories.

First, Christ himself precludes the possibility that a Christian could be inhabited by demons. Using the illustration of a house, Jesus asks, "How can anyone enter a strong man's house and carry off his possessions unless he first ties up the strong man?" (Matthew 12:29). In the case of a demon-possessed person, the strong man is obviously the devil. In a Spirit-indwelt believer, however, the strong man is God. The force of Christ's argument leads inexorably to the conclusion that, in order for demons to possess believers, they would first have to bind the one who occupies them—namely God himself!

Furthermore, I discovered an equally airtight argument against Christian demonization in the Gospel of John. The Jews once again were accusing Jesus of being demon-possessed. Rather than circumvent their accusations, Jesus condescends to reach out to his accusers with reason. The essence of his argument is "I am not possessed by a demon" because "I honor my Father" (John 8:49). The point is impossible to miss: Being demon-possessed and honoring God are mutually exclusive categories.

Finally, Scripture does not contain a single credible example of a demonized believer. Instead, the consistent teaching of the Bible is that Christians cannot be controlled against their wills through demonic inhabitation. The principle is foolproof. If you are a follower of Christ, the King himself indwells you. And you can rest assured that "the one who is in you is greater than the one who is in the world" (1 John 4:4).

For further study, see Hank Hanegraaff, *The Covering: God's Plan to Protect You from Evil* (Nashville: W Publishing, 2002).

1 JOHN 4:4

"You, dear children, are from God and have overcome them, because the one who is in you is greater than the one who is in the world."

DOES SATAN HAVE ACCESS TO OUR MINDS?

While we would greatly overestimate Satan's power by supposing that he can interact directly with us in a physical sense, an equal and opposite error would be to suppose that he does not have access to our minds.

First, while Satan cannot read our minds he can influence our thoughts. Thus, the Bible instructs us to "put on the full armor of God so that you can take your stand against the devil's schemes" (Ephesians 6:11). Without it, you are a guaranteed casualty in the invisible war; with it, you are invincible. Spiritual warfare is waged against invisible beings that personify the extremities of evil. And their weapons are spiritual, not physical. While they cannot bite us physically, violate us sexually, or cause us to levitate, they can tempt us to cheat, steal, and lie.

Furthermore, it is crucial to note that if we open the door to Satan by failing to put on the full armor of God, he does, as it were, sit on our shoulders and whisper into our ears. The whisper cannot be discerned with the physical ear; it can, however, penetrate "the ear" of the mind. We cannot explain how such communication takes place any more than we can explain how our immaterial minds can cause the physical synapses of the brain to fire. But that such mind-to-mind communication takes place is indisputable. If it were not so, the devil could not have tempted Judas to betray his Master, seduced Ananias and Sapphira to deceive Peter, or incited David to take a census.

Finally, while fallen angels are not material beings and thus cannot interact with us directly in the physical sense, they are as real as the very flesh upon our bones. No doubt much to the devil's delight we often depict him as either a cartoonish clown, with an elongated tail, red tights, and a pitchfork—or as a cultural caricature. Far from silly or stupid, however, Satan appears as a cosmopolitan angel of enlightenment. He knows full well that without our spiritual armor we are but pawns in a devil's game.

In the final analysis, the whole of Scripture informs us that spiritual warfare is the battle for the mind.

*The weapons we fight with
are not the weapons of the
world. On the contrary, they
have divine power to demolish
strongholds. We demolish
arguments and every pretension
that sets itself up against the
knowledge of God, and we take
captive every thought
to make it obedient to Christ.*

—2 CORINTHIANS 10:4-5

For further study, see Hank Hanegraaff, *The Covering: God's Plan to Protect You from Evil* (Nashville: W Publishing Group, 2002); and C. S. Lewis, *The Screwtape Letters* (New York: Macmillan, 1982).

EPHESIANS 6:12–13

"For our struggle is not against flesh and blood, but against the rulers, against the authorities, against the powers of this dark world and against the spiritual forces of evil in the heavenly realms. Therefore put on the full armor of God, so that when the day of evil comes, you may be able to stand your ground, and after you have done everything, to stand."

SATAN HAS ACCESS TO OUR MINDS
THROUGH WHAT WE PUT INTO OUR MINDS.

"Do not be anxious about anything, but in everything, by prayer and petition, with thanksgiving, present your requests to God. And the peace of God, which transcends all understanding, will guard your hearts and your minds in Christ Jesus.

"Finally, brothers, whatever is true, whatever is noble, whatever is right, whatever is pure, whatever is lovely, whatever is admirable—if anything is excellent or praiseworthy—think about such things. Whatever you have learned or received or heard from me, or seen in me—put it into practice. And the God of peace will be with you."

—PHILIPPIANS 4:6–9

26

IS SATAN ALWAYS THE CAUSE OF SICKNESS?

f you tune into Christian television on virtually any given day you can hear faith healers screaming at satanic spirits of sicknesses ranging from asthma to arthritis. But is Satan really behind every sickness?

First, while Scripture makes it clear that Satan is often the *agent* of sickness, he is not always the *author* of sickness. Sometimes God is. For example, in Exodus 4:11 God himself asks the rhetorical question "Who gave man his mouth? Who makes him deaf or dumb? Who gives him sight or makes him blind? Is it not I, the LORD?" In 2 Kings 15:5 we read the well-known story of the Lord striking King Azariah with a skin disease from which he suffered till the day he died. And in Luke, the angel of the Lord came directly from God's presence to strike Zechariah with an affliction because he doubted God's word regarding the birth of John the Baptist (Luke 1:19–20).

Furthermore, we live in a cursed creation in which aging is the primary sickness of humanity.

Thus, humanity's fall into a life of constant sin terminated by death, rather than Satan, is by far the primary cause of sickness. As we get older we all get wrinkles, some of us need glasses, our muscles get shorter, and eventually we all die. Since the fall of humankind, both the righteous and the unrighteous have been subject to sickness and disease. Job, who is affirmed by Scripture as a great man of faith, was covered with painful sores from the soles of his feet to the top of his head (Job 2:7). Paul confessed to the Galatians that he preached the gospel to them for the first time because of a "bodily illness" (Galatians 4:13). Timothy was called Paul's "son in the faith" (1 Timothy 1:2) yet he suffered from frequent stomach problems (1 Timothy 5:23). And Elisha was blessed with a "double-portion anointing," yet he suffered and died a sick man (2 Kings 13:14).

Finally, it is crucial to note that this world is under the sovereign control of God, not Satan. Thus, we can rest assured that even in sickness and suffering all things work together for good to those who love God and are called according to his purpose (Romans 8:28). For the child of God, the hope is not perfect health in this lifetime but a resurrected body in the life to come. As John the

Humanity's fall into a life
of constant sin terminated by death,
rather than Satan,
is the primary cause of sickness.

apostle so beautifully put it, "'There will be no more death or mourning or crying or pain, for the old order of things has passed away' He who was seated on the throne said, 'I am making everything new!'" (Revelation 21:4–5).

For further study, see Hank Hanegraaff, *Christianity in Crisis* (Eugene, Ore.: Harvest House Publishers, 1993).

EXODUS 4:11, NAS

"The LORD said to him, "Who has made man's mouth? Or who makes him mute or deaf, or seeing or blind? Is it not I, the LORD?""

27

DID DEMONS HAVE SEXUAL RELATIONS
WITH WOMEN IN GENESIS 6:4?

enesis 6:4 is one of the most controversial passages in the Bible. As with any difficult section of Scripture, it has been open to a wide variety of interpretations. It is my conviction however, that those who hold consistently to a biblical worldview must reject the notion that women and demons can engage in sexual relations. I reject this interjection of pagan superstition into the Scriptures for the following reasons.

First and foremost, the notion that demons can "produce" real bodies and have real sex with real women would invalidate Jesus' argument for the authenticity of his resurrection. Jesus assured his disciples that "a spirit does not have flesh and bones, as you see I have" (Luke 24:39, NKJV). If indeed a demon could produce flesh and bones Jesus' argument would not only be flawed, it would be misleading. In fact, it might be logically argued that the disciples did not see the postresurrection appearances of Christ but rather a demon masquerading as the resurrected Christ.

Furthermore, demons are nonsexual nonphysical beings and as such are incapable of having sexual relations and producing physical offspring. To say that demons can create bodies with DNA and fertile sperm is to say that demons have creative power—which is an exclusively divine prerogative. If demons could have sex with women in ancient times, we would have no assurance they could not do so in modern times. Nor would we have any guarantee that the people we encounter every day are fully human. While a biblical worldview does allow for fallen angels to *possess* unsaved human beings, it does not support the notion that a demon-possessed person can produce offspring that are part-demon, part-human. Genesis 1 makes it clear that all of God's living creations are designed to reproduce "according to their own kinds."

Finally, the mutant theory creates serious questions pertaining to the spiritual accountability of hypothetical demon-humans and their relation to humanity's redemption. Angels rebelled individually, are judged individually, and are offered no plan of redemption in Scripture. On the other hand, humans fell corporately in Adam, are judged corporately in Adam, and are redeemed corporately through Jesus

Christ. We have no biblical way of determining what category the demon-humans would fit into—whether they would be judged as angels or as men, or more significantly, whether they might even be among those for whom Christ died.

I believe the better interpretation is that "sons of God" simply refers to the godly descendants of Seth, and "daughters of men" to the ungodly descendants of Cain. Their cohabitation caused humanity to fall into such utter depravity that God said: "I will wipe mankind, whom I have created, from the face of the earth—men and animals, and creatures that move along the ground, and birds of the air—for I am grieved that I have made them. But Noah found favor in the eyes of the Lord" (Genesis 6:7–8).

For further study, see Hank Hanegraaff, "Questions and Answers: Genesis 6:4," available from CRI at www.equip.org; see also Gleason L. Archer, *New International Encyclopedia of Bible Difficulties* (Grand Rapids: Zondervan, 1982), 79–80.

GENESIS 6:4

"The Nephilim were on the earth in those days—and also afterward—when the sons of God went to the daughters of men and had children by them. They were the heroes of old, men of renown."

28

IS IT EVER MORALLY PERMISSIBLE TO LIE?

I n the interest of truth, I should first disclose the fact that Christian theologians are divided on this subject. Some—like Saint Augustine—believed that it is never permissible to lie. Others—like Dietrich Bonhoeffer, who had ample time to contemplate this issue from the perspective of a Nazi prison cell—held that under certain circumstances lying was not only morally permissible but morally mandated. Thus, Bonhoeffer advocated deceiving the enemy in circumstances of war, and he had no compunction about lying in order to facilitate escape for Jews facing extermination.

Furthermore, while the Bible never condones lying *qua* lying (lying for the sake of lying), it does condone lying in order to preserve a higher moral imperative. For example, Rahab purposed to deceive (the lesser moral law) in order to preserve the lives of two Jewish spies (the higher moral law). Likewise, a Christian father today should not hesitate to lie in order to protect his wife and daughters from the imminent threat of rape or murder.

Finally, there is a difference between *lying* and *not telling the truth*. This is not merely a matter of semantics; it is a matter of substance. By way of analogy, there is a difference between unjustified and justified homicide. Murder is unjustified homicide and is always wrong. Not every instance of killing a person, however, is murder. Capital punishment and self-defense occasion justified homicide. Similarly, in the case of a lie (Annanias and Sapphira, Acts 5) there is an unjustified discrepancy between what you believe and what you say, and so *lying* is always wrong. But *not telling the truth* in order to preserve a higher moral law (Rahab, Joshua 2) may well be the right thing to do and thus is not actually a lie.

For further study, see Norman L. Geisler, *Christian Ethics: Options and Issues* (Grand Rapids: Baker Book House, 1989), chapter 7.

JOSHUA 2:3–6
"The king of Jericho sent this message to Rahab: 'Bring out the men who came to you and entered your house, because they have come to spy out the whole land.' But the woman had taken the two men and hidden them. She said, 'Yes, the men came to me,

*but I did not know where they had come from.
At dusk, when it was time to close the city gate, the
men left. I don't know which way they went. Go after
them quickly. You may catch up with them.' (But she
had taken them up to the roof and hidden them under
the stalks of flax she had laid out on the roof.)"*

WHAT IS ABORTION?

T hose who continue to fight legislation restricting abortion are in reality *not* "pro-choice." Rather, they are singularly "pro-murder." While rhetoric has served to camouflage the carnage of abortion, it remains the *painful killing of an innocent human being.*

First, abortion is *painful* in that the methods employed to kill a preborn child involve burning, smothering, dismembering, and crushing. And such procedures are executed on live babies who have not been specifically anesthetized.

Furthermore, abortion involves *killing.* The zygote, which fulfills the criteria needed to establish the existence of biological life (metabolism, development, the ability to react to stimuli, and cell reproduction), is indeed terminated. In *Woman and the New Race,* Planned Parenthood founder Margaret Sanger tacitly acknowledged this point when she wrote: "The most merciful thing a large family can do for one of its infant members is to kill it."

Abortion—

the painful killing

of an innocent

human being.

Finally, abortion kills innocent *human beings*. The child that is terminated is the product of human parents and has a totally distinct human genetic code. Although the emerging embryo does not have a fully developed personality, it does have complete personhood from the moment of conception. Thus, far from deserving capital punishment, these innocent humans deserve care and protection.

Thankfully, in God's economy there is hope for those who have experienced the ravages of abortion. Not only can they receive God's forgiveness in the here and now, but they can yet look forward to the ecstasy of reuniting with their unborn loved ones in eternity.

For further study, see Francis J. Beckwith, *Politically Correct Death: Answering the Arguments for Abortion Rights*, (Grand Rapids: Baker Books, 1993).

PSALM 139:13–16
"For you created my inmost being; you knit me together in my mother's womb. I praise you because I am fearfully and wonderfully made; your works are wonderful, I know that full well. My frame was not hidden from you when I was made in the secret place. When I was woven together in the depths of the earth, your eyes saw my unformed body."

CAN HUMAN CLONING BE HARMONIZED
WITH A CHRISTIAN WORLDVIEW?

s has been well said, "The only thing necessary for evil to triumph is for good men to do nothing." The stark reality of this sentiment was borne out in 1973 when Christians quietly passed by a major battle in the war against abortion. Two and a half decades later, the far-reaching impact of that loss is being felt in a raging debate over human cloning. While Pandora's box is already open, Christians must do all that is permissible to prevent a human clone from emerging.

First, the issues concerning cloning and abortion are inextricably woven together. In other words, the prevailing logic that permits a woman to terminate the life of a child in the womb may well equally apply to cloning. For example, if defects were detected in developing clones, abortion might well be the solution of choice.

Furthermore, producing a human clone would of necessity require experimentation on hundreds if not thousands of live human embryos. Thus, the entire process would be the moral equivalent of human experiments carried out by Nazi scientists under Adolf Hitler.

Finally, it should be noted that cloning has serious implications regarding what constitutes a family. While children are the result of spousal reproduction, clones are essentially the result of scientific replication. Which raises the question: Who owns the clone? It is terrifying to think that the first human clone might well be owned and operated by the very scientists who conduct such ghastly experiments.

For further study, see Hank Hanegraaff, *The F.A.C.E. That Demonstrates the Farce of Evolution* (Nashville: Word Publishing, 1998), Appendix E "Human Cloning" and also Appendix D "Annihilating Abortion Arguments"; see also The Center for Bioethics and Human Dignity, 2065 Half Day Road, Bannockburn, IL 60015, www.cbhd.org.

JOB 33:4
"The Spirit of God has made me; the breath of the Almighty gives me life."

Is Capital Punishment Biblical?

hristians who believe in capital punishment and those who do not both use the Bible to buttress their beliefs. So, what does the Bible really teach regarding capital punishment?

To begin with, it should be noted that in the very first book of the Bible God clearly communicates his position with respect to capital punishment: "Whoever sheds the blood of man, by man shall his blood be shed; for in the image of God has God made man" (Genesis 9:6). It is instructive to note that this passage not only predates the Mosaic Law, but it demands universal adherence to the sanctity of life.

Furthermore, in Exodus 21 and Deuteronomy 19 the Bible reaffirms God's perspective on capital punishment by underscoring the principle of "life for life." To murder a person who is made in the image of God is not only to show contempt for the apex of God's creation but also to show contempt for the Creator himself. Thus, while capital punishment may be reprehensible from a secular perspective, it is basic to a biblical worldview.

Finally, capital punishment is implicitly validated in the New Testament. Jesus acknowledged the legitimacy of capital punishment before Pilate (John 19:11), as did the apostle Paul before the Roman Governor Festus (Acts 25:11). Not only so, but one of the thieves crucified with Christ had the candor to confess, "We are punished justly, for we are getting what our deeds deserve" (Luke 23:41). Moreover, Romans 13 implies that the failure of the governing authorities to apply the "sword"—the Roman symbol for capital punishment—exalts evil and eradicates equity.

In short, God instituted capital punishment in the earliest stages of human civilization before the Mosaic Law, and capital punishment is never abrogated by Jesus or the Apostles. Thus, capital punishment appears to be an enduring moral principle undergirding the sanctity of life.

For further study, see Hank Hanegraaff "Karla Faye Tucker and Capital Punishment," available from CRI at www.equip.org; See also J. Daryl Charles, "Sentiments as Social Justice: The Ethics of Capital Punishment," *Christian Research Journal*, Spring/Summer 1994.

"And from each man too, I will demand an accounting for the life of his fellow man. Whoever sheds the blood of man, by man shall his blood be shed; for in the image of God has God made man."

DOES THE BIBLE PROMOTE SLAVERY?

A myth propped up by secular skeptics is that Scripture sanctions slavery. Nothing could be farther from the truth.

First, it should be noted that far from extolling the virtues of slavery, the Bible denounces slavery as sin. The New Testament goes so far as to put slave traders in the same category as murderers, adulterers, perverts, and liars (1 Timothy 1:10).

Furthermore, slavery within the Old Testament context was sanctioned due to economic realities rather than racial or sexual prejudices. Because bankruptcy laws did not exist, people would *voluntarily* sell themselves into slavery. A craftsman could thus use his skills in servitude to discharge a debt. Even a convicted thief could make restitution by serving as a slave (Exodus 22:3).

Finally, while the Bible as a whole recognizes the reality of slavery it never promotes the practice of slavery. In fact, it was the application of biblical principles that ultimately led to the overthrow of slavery, both in ancient Israel and in the United

States of America. Israel's liberation from slavery in Egypt became the model for the liberation of slaves in general. In America, many are beginning to wake up to the liberating biblical truth that *all* people are created by God with innate equality (Genesis 1:27; Acts 17:26–28; Galatians 3:28).

For further study, see Paul Copan, *That's Just Your Interpretation: Responding to Skeptics Who Challenge Your Faith* (Grand Rapids: Baker Books, 2001), 171–178. See also Hank Hanegraaff, "President Bartlett's Fallacious Diatribe." Available from CRI at www.equip.org.

1 Timothy 1:8–11

"We know that the law is good if one
uses it properly. We also know that law is made not
for the righteous but for lawbreakers and rebels,
the ungodly and sinful, the unholy and irreligious;
for those who kill their fathers
or mothers, for murderers, for adulterers and perverts,
for slave traders and liars and perjurers—
and for whatever else is contrary to the sound doctrine
that conforms to the glorious gospel
of the blessed God, which he entrusted to me."

Were you a slave when you were called? Don't let it trouble you—although if you can gain your freedom, do so. For he who was a slave when he was called by the Lord is the Lord's freedman; similarly, he who was a free man when he was called is Christ's slave. You were bought at a price; do not become slaves of men.

—1 CORINTHIANS 7:21–23

– 3 3 –

DOES HOMOSEXUALITY DEMONSTRATE
THAT THE BIBLE IS
ANTIQUATED AND IRRELEVANT?

A popular sentiment today is that the Bible is increasingly irrelevant in a modern age of scientific enlightenment. Thus, when the Scripture's condemnation of homosexuality is referenced it is not uncommon to see expressions of polite exasperation etched on the faces of the masses. After all, the Bible not only condemns homosexuality but also clearly teaches that Sabbath breakers must be put to death (Exodus 35:2).

First, it should be noted that while Sabbath-breaking had serious ramifications within ancient Israel, it is not a precedent for executing people today. Not only are we no longer under the civil and ceremonial laws of a Jewish theocratic form of government, but as the apostle Paul explains, the symbolism of the law has been fulfilled in Christ (Galatians 3:13–14). In his letter to the Colossian Christians, Paul underscores the Christian's freedom from adherence to Sabbath laws by pointing out that "these are a shadow of the things that were to come; the reality, however, is found in Christ" (Colossians 2:17). Thus, there is an obvious difference between enduring moral principles regarding homosexuality and temporary civil and ceremonial laws relegated to a particular historical context.

Furthermore, we would do well to recognize that the God of the Bible does not condemn homosexuality in an arbitrary and capricious fashion. Rather he carefully defines the borders of human sexuality so that our joy may be complete. It does not require an advanced degree in physiology to appreciate the fact that the human body is not designed for homosexual relationships. Spurious slogans and sound bites do not change the scientific reality that homosexual relationships are devastating not only from a psychological but also from a physiological perspective.

Finally, far from being irrelevant and antiquated, the Bible's warnings regarding homosexuality are eerily relevant and up to date. The book of Romans aptly describes both the perversion and the penalty: "Their women exchanged natural relations for unnatural ones. In the same way the men also abandoned natural relations with women and were inflamed with lust for one another. Men committed indecent acts with other men, and *received in themselves the due penalty for their perversion*" (Romans 1:26–27, emphasis added). It would be difficult to miss the relationship between Paul's words and the current healthcare holocaust. More people already have died worldwide from AIDS than the United States of America has lost in all its wars combined. This is but the tip of an insidious iceberg. The homosexual lifestyle causes a host of complications including hemorrhoids, prostate damage, and infectious fissures. And even that merely scratches the surface. Nonviral infections transmitted through homosexual activity include gonorrhea, chlamydia, and syphilis. Viral infections involve condylomata, herpes, and hepatitis A and B.

While there are attendant moral and medical problems with sexual promiscuity in general, it would be homophobic in the extreme to obscure the scientific realities concerning homosexuality. It is a hate crime of unparalleled proportions to attempt to keep a whole segment of the population in the dark concerning such issues. Thus, far from demonstrating that the Bible is out of step with the times, its warnings regarding homosexuality demonstrate that it is as relevant today as it was in the beginning.

The God of the Bible does not condemn homosexuality in an arbitrary and capricious fashion. Rather he carefully defines the borders of human sexuality so that our joy may be complete.

For further study, see Joe Dallas, *A Strong Delusion: Confronting the "Gay Christian" Movement* (Eugene, Ore.: Harvest House Publishers, 1996). See also Hank Hanegraaff, "President Bartlett's Fallacious Diatribe," available at www.equip.org.

ROMANS 1:26–27

"Even their women exchanged natural relations for unnatural ones. In the same way the men also abandoned natural relations with women and were inflamed with lust for one another. Men committed indecent acts with other men, and received in themselves the due penalty for their perversion."

O LORD, you have searched me
and you know me.
You know when I sit and when I rise;
you perceive my thoughts from afar.
You discern my going out and my lying down;
you are familiar with all my ways.
Before a word is on my tongue
you know it completely, O LORD.

You hem me in—behind and before;
you have laid your hand upon me.
Such knowledge is too wonderful for me,
too lofty for me to attain.

Where can I go from your Spirit?
Where can I flee from your presence?
If I go up to the heavens, you are there;
if I make my bed in the depths, you are there.
If I rise on the wings of the dawn,
if I settle on the far side of the sea,
even there your hand will guide me,
your right hand will hold me fast.

If I say, "Surely the darkness will hide me
and the light become night around me,"
even the darkness will not be dark to you;
the night will shine like the day,
for darkness is as light to you.

For you created my inmost being;
you knit me together in my mother's womb.
I praise you because I am fearfully and
wonderfully made;
your works are wonderful,
I know that full well.
My frame was not hidden from you
when I was made in the secret place.
When I was woven together in the depths of the earth,
your eyes saw my unformed body.
All the days ordained for me
were written in your book
before one of them came to be.

How precious to me are your thoughts, O God!
How vast is the sum of them!
Were I to count them,
they would outnumber the grains of sand.
When I awake,
I am still with you.

If only you would slay the wicked, O God!
Away from me, you bloodthirsty men!
They speak of you with evil intent;
your adversaries misuse your name.
Do I not hate those who hate you, O LORD,
and abhor those who rise up against you?
I have nothing but hatred for them;
I count them my enemies.

Search me, O God, and know my heart;
test me and know my anxious thoughts.
See if there is any offensive way in me,
and lead me in the way everlasting.

IS CREMATION CONSISTENT
WITH THE CHRISTIAN WORLDVIEW?

remation has become an increasingly popular means for disposing of the dead. In fact, by the year 2010, it is estimated that one-third of all Americans will cremate their loved ones. While those who opt for cremation often do so on the basis of emotional, economical, or ecological considerations, there are compelling reasons for Christians to choose burial.

First, Scripture clearly favors burial over cremation. The Old Testament pattern was always burial except in highly unusual circumstances. Likewise, in the New Testament Paul equates baptism with both burial and resurrection (Romans 6:4).

Furthermore, burial symbolizes the promise of resurrection by anticipating the preservation of the body. Cremation, however, better symbolizes the pagan worldview of reincarnation. While resurrectionists look forward to the restoration of the body, reincarnationists look forward to being relieved from their bodies.

*While God has
no problem resurrecting
the cremated,
cremation does not point to the
resurrection of God.*

Finally, burial highlights the sanctity of the body. In the Christian worldview, the body is significant in that it has numerical identity to the resurrected body. Thus, while God has no problem resurrecting the cremated, cremation does not point to the resurrection of God.

For further study, see Hank Hanegraaff, *Resurrection* (Nashville: Word Publishing, 2000), chapter 15; and Norman L. Geisler and Douglas E. Potter, "From Ashes to Ashes: Is Burial the Only Christian Option?" Available from CRI at www.equip.org.

ROMANS 6:4
"We were therefore buried with him through baptism into death in order that, just as Christ was raised from the dead through the glory of the Father, we too may live a new life."

HOW OLD WILL WE BE IN HEAVEN?

cripture does not specifically address the issue of apparent age; however it does provide glorious insights concerning the state of our resurrected bodies.

First, when God created Adam and Eve in Eden, he created them with apparent age and in the prime of life. Additionally, Jesus died and was resurrected at the prime of his physical development. Thus we are justified in believing that whether we die in infancy, in our prime, or in old age, we will be resurrected physically mature and perfect, as God originally intended.

Furthermore, our DNA is programmed in such a way that at a particular point we reach optimal development from a functional perspective. For the most part, it appears that we reach this stage somewhere in our twenties or thirties. Prior to this stage, the development of our bodies (anabolism) exceeds the devolution of our bodies (catabolism). From this point on, the rate of breakdown exceeds the rate of buildup, which eventually leads to physical death. All of this is to say that if the blueprint for our glorified bodies is in the DNA, then it would stand to reason that our bodies will be resurrected at the optimal stage of development determined by our DNA.

Finally, one thing can be stated with certainty—in heaven, there will be no deformities. The body, tarnished by humanity's fall into a life of constant sin terminated by death, will be utterly transformed. You will be the perfect you, and I will be the perfect me. Indeed, in heaven "there will be no more death or mourning or crying or pain, for the old order of things has passed away" (Revelation 21:4).

For further study see, Peter J. Kreeft, *Everything You Ever Wanted to Know About Heaven, but Never Dreamed of Asking* (San Francisco: Ignatius Press, 1990).

ISAIAH 35:5–6
*"Then will the eyes of the blind be opened
and the ears of the deaf unstopped.
Then will the lame leap like a deer, and the
mute tongue shout for joy.
Water will gush forth in the wilderness
and streams in the desert."*

WILL THERE BE ANIMALS IN HEAVEN?

Scripture does not conclusively tell us whether our pets will make it to heaven. However, the Bible does provide us with some significant clues regarding whether or not animals will inhabit the new heaven and the new earth.

First, animals populated the Garden of Eden. Thus, there is a precedent for believing that animals will populate Eden Restored as well. Animals are among God's most creative creations. Thus, it would seem incredible that he would banish such wonders in heaven.

Furthermore, while we cannot say for certain that the pets we enjoy today will be "resurrected" in eternity, I am not willing to preclude the possibility. Some of the keenest thinkers from C. S. Lewis to Peter Kreeft are not only convinced that animals in general but that pets in particular will be restored in the resurrection. If God resurrected our pets it would be in total keeping with His overwhelming grace and goodness.

Finally, the Scriptures from first to last suggest that animals have souls. Both Moses in Genesis and John in Revelation communicate that the Creator endowed animals with souls. In the original languages of Genesis 1:20 and Revelation 8:9, *nephesh* and *psyche* respectively refer to the essence of life or soul. Not until Descartes and Hobbes and the Enlightenment did people think otherwise about animals. However, because the soul of an animal is qualitatively different from the soul of a human there is reasonable doubt that it can survive the death of its body. One thing is certain: Scripture provides us with sufficient precedence for believing that animals will inhabit the new heaven and new earth. In the words of Isaiah: "The wolf will live with the lamb, the leopard will lie down with the goat, the calf and the lion and the yearling together; and a little child will lead them" (Isaiah 11:6).

For further study see, Hank Hanegraaff, *Resurrection* (Nashville: Word Publishing, 2000), chapter 13.

PSALM 145:13
"Your kingdom is an everlasting kingdom,
and your dominion endures through all generations.
The LORD is faithful to all his promises
and loving toward all he has made."

WILL THERE BE SEX IN HEAVEN?

What do you see in your mind's eye when the word "sex" is mentioned? An image of Madonna on MTV? A James Bond movie? *Cosmopolitan* magazine? Or does your mind immediately flash from sex to Scripture? Trust me! When it comes to sex, *Playboy* cannot hold a candle to Scripture. If you think that's an overstatement, just read a few pages of Solomon's Song of Songs. Tragically, what the Creator purposed to be pristine and pure, the creation has prostituted and perverted. But that is not where the story ends! God does not arbitrarily *remove* things—he *redeems* them. So will there be sex in the resurrection? Yes and no—it all depends on what you mean by sex.

First, by nature or essence we are sexual beings. Thus, sex is not just something you *do*. Sex is what you *are!* The foremost reason we can say with certainty that sex will exist in the resurrection is that sex is not merely a word that describes an erotic experience, it is what we are by essence—in the beginning God created us male and female (Genesis 1:27) and that is likely how it always will be.

Furthermore, we can safely surmise that there will be *sexuality* in heaven because heaven will personify enjoyment. Men and women will enjoy each another—not in a mere physical sense but in a metaphysical sense. This reality is virtually impossible for a crass materialist to grasp. The materialist views sexual pleasure as a function of fitting body parts together. Christians, however, see humanity as a psychosomatic unity of both body and soul. Thus, we are not solely sexual *somas* (bodies), we are sexual souls as well. In heaven, the pleasure that the male and female sex will experience in one another will be infinitely magnified, because in eternity our earthly conception of sex will have been eclipsed. In place of selfishness, we will take pleasure in selflessness.

Finally, we can safely assume that there will be sex in eternity because God created sex in Eden *before* humanity's fall into a life of constant sin terminated by death. Thus, in Eden restored we can rest assured that God will not *remove* our sexual nature, rather He will *redeem* it. In the new heaven and new earth, sex will no longer be for the purpose of procreation. Nor will it involve sexual intercourse—for "at the resurrection people will

*In Eden restored we can rest
assured that God will not remove
our sexual nature,
rather He will redeem it.*

neither marry nor be given in marriage; they will be like the angels in heaven" (Matthew 22:30). In heaven we will experience a kind of spiritual intercourse that eludes our grasp on earth. In paradise, romance subverted will become romance sublime. It will be agape-driven rather than animal-driven. In Eden Restored our sexual bodies and sexual souls will fly full and free, unfettered by the stain of selfishness and sin.

Will there be sex in the resurrection? Again, yes and no. Yes, there will be *sexuality* in heaven in that *we* will be in heaven—and *we* by our very nature are sexual beings. And no, there is no warrant for believing there will be *sex* in heaven in terms of the physical act.

For further study, see Hank Hanegraaff, *Resurrection* (Nashville: Word Publishing), Chapter 17. See also Peter J. Kreeft, *Everything You Ever Wanted to Know About Heaven, but Never Dreamed of Asking* (San Francisco: Ignatius Press, 1990).

GENESIS 1:27
*"So God created man in his own image,
in the image of God he created him; male and
female he created them."*

If Heaven Is Perfect,
Won't It Be Perfectly Boring?

An all-too-prevalent perception in Christianity and the culture is that heaven is going to be one big bore. That, however, is far from true. Rather, heaven will be a place of continuous learning, growth, and development. By nature, humans are finite, and that is how it always will be. While we will have an incredible capacity to learn, we will never come to the end of learning.

To begin with, we will never exhaust exploring our Creator. God by nature is infinite and we are limited. Thus, what we now merely apprehend about the Creator we will spend an eternity seeking to comprehend. Imagine finally beginning to get a handle on how God is one in nature and three in person. Imagine exploring the depths of God's love, wisdom, and holiness. Imagine forever growing in our capacities to fathom his immensity, immutability, and incomprehensibility. And to top it all off, the more we come to know him, the more there will be to know.

"These are they who have come out of the
great tribulation; they have washed
their robes and made them white in
the blood of the Lamb. Therefore,
they are before the throne of God
and serve him day and night in
his temple;
and he who sits on the throne will spread
his tent over them.
Never again will they hunger;
never again will they thirst.
The sun will not beat upon them,
nor any scorching heat.
For the Lamb at the center of the throne
will be their shepherd;
he will lead them to springs of
living water.
And God will wipe away every tear from
their eyes."

—REVELATION 7:15-17

Furthermore, we will never come to the end of exploring fellow Christians. Our ability to appreciate one another will be enhanced exponentially. Imagine being able to love another human being without even a tinge of selfishness. Imagine appreciating, no, *reveling* in the exalted capacities and station that God bestows on another without so much as a modicum of jealousy.

Finally, we will never come to an end of exploring the Creator's creative handiwork. The universe literally will be our playground. Even if we were capable of exhausting the "new heaven and new earth" (Revelation 21:1), God could create brand new vistas for us to explore.

Will heaven be perfect? Absolutely. Will it be boring? Absolutely not! We will learn without error—but make no mistake about it, *we will learn, we will grow, and we will develop.* Far from being dead and dull, heaven will be an exhilarating, exciting experience that will never come to an end.

For further study, see Peter J. Kreeft, *Everything You Ever Wanted to Know About Heaven, but Never Dreamed of Asking* (San Francisco: Ignatius Press, 1990).

"You have made known to me the path of life;
you will fill me with joy in your presence,
with eternal pleasures at your right hand."

—39—

CAN CHANCE ACCOUNT FOR THE UNIVERSE?

stronaut Guy Gardner, who has seen the earth from the perspective of the moon, points out that "the more we learn and see about the universe the more we come to realize that the most ideally suited place for life within the entire solar system is the planet we call home." In other words, life on earth was designed by a benevolent Creator rather than directed by blind chance.

First, consider the ideal temperatures on planet Earth—not duplicated on any other known planet in the universe. If we were closer to the sun, we would fry. If we were farther away, we would freeze.

Furthermore, ocean tides, which are caused by the gravitational pull of the moon, play a crucial role in our survival. If the moon were significantly larger, thereby having a stronger gravitational pull, devastating tidal waves would submerge large areas of land. If the moon were smaller, tidal motion would cease, and the oceans would stagnate and die.

Finally, consider plain old tap water. The solid state of most substances is denser than their liquid state, but the opposite is true for water, which explains why ice floats rather than sinks. If water were like virtually any other liquid, it would freeze from the bottom up rather than from the top down, killing aquatic life, destroying the oxygen supply, and making earth uninhabitable.

From the temperatures to the tides and the tap water, and myriad other characteristics that we so easily take for granted, the earth is an unparalleled planetary masterpiece. Like Handel's *Messiah* or da Vinci's *Last Supper*, it should never be carelessly pawned off as the result of blind evolutionary processes.

For further study, see R.C. Sproul, *Not A Chance: The Myth of Chance in Modern Science and Cosmology* (Grand Rapids: Baker Book House, 1994).

Genesis 1:1

*"In the beginning
God created the heavens and the earth."*

The earth is an unparalleled planetary masterpiece.

40

HOW MANY EXPLANATIONS ARE THERE FOR THE EXISTENCE OF OUR UNIVERSE?

Philosophical naturalism—the worldview undergirding evolutionism—can provide only three explanations.

First, the universe is merely an illusion. This notion carries little weight in an age of scientific enlightenment.

Second, the universe sprang from nothing. This proposition flies in the face of both the laws of cause and effect and energy conservation. As has been well said, "Nothing comes from nothing, nothing ever could." Or, to put it another way, there simply are no free lunches. The conditions that hold true in this universe prevent any possibility of matter springing out of nothing.

Third, the universe eternally existed. The law of entropy, which predicts that a universe that has eternally existed would have died an "eternity ago" of heat loss, devastates this hypothesis.

There is, however, one other possibility. It is found in the first chapter of the first book of the

Bible: "In the beginning God created the heavens and the earth." In an age of empirical science, nothing could be more certain, clear, or correct.

For further study, see James W. Sire, *The Universe Next Door: A Basic Worldview Catalog*, third ed. (Downers Grove, Ill.: InterVarsity Press, 1997); C. S. Lewis, *Mere Christianity* (New York: Macmillan, 1952).

ROMANS 1:20

"For since the creation of the world God's invisible qualities—his eternal power and divine nature— have been clearly seen, being understood from what has been made, so that men are without excuse."

41

WHO MADE GOD?

one of the arguments forwarded by philosophical naturalism—(1) the universe is merely an illusion; (2) the universe sprang from nothing; (3) the universe eternally existed—satisfactorily account for the existence of the universe. Logically, we can turn only to the possibility that "God created the heavens and the earth" (Genesis 1:1). If that's the case, however, it immediately brings up the question—Who made God?

First, unlike the universe, which according to modern science had a beginning, God is infinite and eternal. Thus, as an infinite eternal being, God logically can be demonstrated to be the uncaused First Cause.

Furthermore, to suppose that because the universe had a cause, the cause of the universe must have had a cause simply leads to a logical dead end. An infinite regression of finite causes does not answer the question of *source*; it merely makes the *effects* more numerous.

Finally, simple logic dictates that the universe is not merely an illusion; it did not spring out of nothing (nothing comes from nothing; nothing ever could); and it has not eternally existed (the law of entropy predicts that a universe that has eternally existed would have died an "eternity ago" of heat loss). Thus, the only philosophically plausible possibility that remains is that the universe was made by an unmade Cause greater than itself.

For further study, see Paul Copan, *That's Just Your Interpretation: Responding to Skeptics Who Challenge Your Faith* (Grand Rapids: Baker Books, 2001), 69–73.

PSALM 90:2
*"Before the mountains were born
or you brought forth the earth and the world,
from everlasting to everlasting you are God."*

42

WHAT IS TRUTH?

his is the very question Pontius Pilate asked Jesus. In the irony of the ages, he stood toe to toe with the personification of truth and yet missed its reality. Postmodern people are in much the same position. They stare at truth but fail to recognize its identity.

First, truth is an aspect of the nature of God himself. Thus, to put on truth is to put on Christ. For Christ is "truth" (John 14:6), and Christians are to be the bearers of truth. As Os Guinness explains, Christianity is not true because it works (pragmatism); it is not true because it feels right (subjectivism); it is not true because it is "my truth" (relativism). It is true because it is anchored in the person of Christ.

Furthermore, truth is anything that corresponds to reality. As such, truth does not yield to the size and strength of the latest lobby group. Nor is truth merely a matter of preference or opinion. Rather truth is true even if everyone denies it, and a lie is a lie even if everyone affirms it.

Finally, truth is essential to a realistic worldview. When sophistry, sensationalism, and superstition sabotage truth, our view of reality is seriously skewed. The death of truth spells the death of civilization. However, as Aleksandr Solzhenitsyn discovered, "One word of truth outweighs the entire world."

For further study, see Os Guinness, *Time for Truth* (Grand Rapids: Baker Books, 2000).

JOHN 18:37–38

"'You are a king, then!' said Pilate. Jesus answered, 'You are right in saying I am a king. In fact, for this reason I was born, and for this I came into the world, to testify to the truth. Everyone on the side of truth listens to me.' 'What is truth?' Pilate asked."

— 43 —

WHAT DISTINGUISHES CHRISTIANITY
FROM OTHER RELIGIONS?

 hristianity is unique among the religions of the world for several reasons.

First, unlike other religions, Christianity is rooted in history and evidence. Jesus of Nazareth was born in Bethlehem in Judea during the reign of Caesar Augustus and was put to death by Pontius Pilate, a first century Roman governor. The testimony of his life, death, and resurrection is validated both by credible eyewitness testimony and by credible extra-biblical evidence as well. No other religion can legitimately claim this kind of support from history and evidence.

Furthermore, of all the influential religious leaders of the world (Buddha, Moses, Zoroaster, Krishna, Lao Tzu, Muhammad, Baha'u'llah), only Jesus claimed to be God in human flesh (Mark 14:62). And this was not an empty boast. For through the historically verifiable fact of resurrection, Christ vindicated His claim to deity (Romans 1:4; 1 Corinthians 15:3–8). Other

*Christianity corresponds
with the
reality of our
present condition.*

religions, such as Buddhism and Islam, claim miracles in support of their faith; however, unlike Christianity, such miracles lack historical validation.

Finally, Christianity is unique in that it is a coherent belief structure. Some Christian doctrines may transcend comprehension, however, unlike the claims of other religions, they are never irrational or contradictory. Christianity is also unique in that it cogently accounts for the vast array of phenomena we encounter in everyday life: the human mind, laws of science, laws of logic, ethical norms, justice, love, meaning in life, the problem of evil and suffering, and truth. In other words, Christianity corresponds with the reality of our present condition.

For further study, see James W. Sire, *The Universe Next Door*, 3rd edition (Downers Grove, Ill.: InterVarsity Press, 1997); and Lee Strobel, *The Case for Christ* (Grand Rapids: Zondervan Publishing House, 1998).

2 PETER 1:16

"We did not follow cleverly invented stories when we told you about the power and coming of our Lord Jesus Christ, but we were eyewitnesses of his majesty."

HOW DO WE KNOW THAT THE BIBLE IS DIVINE RATHER THAN HUMAN IN ORIGIN?

T o defend the faith we must be equipped to demonstrate that the Bible is divine rather than human in origin. When we can successfully accomplish this, we can answer a host of other objections by appealing to Scripture.

To begin with, the Bible has stronger manuscript support than any other work of classical history—including Homer, Plato, Aristotle, Caesar, and Tacitus. Equally amazing is the fact that the Bible has been virtually unaltered since the original writing, as is attested by scholars who have compared the earliest extant manuscripts with manuscripts written centuries later. Additionally, the reliability of the Bible is affirmed by the testimony of its authors, who were eyewitnesses—or close associates of eyewitnesses—to the recorded events, and by secular historians who confirm the many events, people, places, and customs chronicled in Scripture.

Furthermore, archaeology is a powerful witness to the accuracy of the New Testament documents.

Repeatedly, comprehensive archaeological fieldwork and careful biblical interpretation affirm the reliability of the Bible. For example, recent archaeological finds have corroborated biblical details surrounding the trial that led to the fatal torment of Jesus Christ—including Pontius Pilate, who ordered Christ's crucifixion, as well as Caiaphas, the high priest who presided over the religious trials of Christ. It is telling when secular scholars must revise their biblical criticisms in light of solid archaeological evidence.

Finally, the Bible records predictions of events that could not be known nor predicted by chance or common sense. For example, the book of Daniel (written before 530 B.C.) accurately predicts the progression of kingdoms from Babylon through the Medo-Persian Empire, the Greek Empire, and then the Roman Empire, culminating in the persecution and suffering of the Jews under Antiochus IV Epiphanes with his desecration of the temple, his untimely death, and freedom for the Jews under Judas Maccabeus (165 B.C.). It is statistically preposterous that any or all of the Bible's specific, detailed prophecies could have been fulfilled through chance, good guessing, or deliberate deceit.

For further study, see Lee Strobel, *The Case for Christ: A Journalist's Personal Investigation of the Evidence for Jesus* (Grand Rapids: Zondervan, 1998).

2 TIMOTHY 3:16

"All Scripture is God-breathed and is useful for teaching, rebuking, correcting and training in righteousness."

45

DON'T ALL RELIGIONS LEAD TO GOD?

Before answering this question, a word of warning is in order: Anyone who answers in the negative may well be ostracized for being narrow-minded and intolerant. That being said, my answer is, "No, not all religions lead to God, and it is incorrect and illogical to maintain that they do."

First, when you begin to examine world religions such as Judaism, Hinduism, and Buddhism, you will immediately recognize that they directly contradict one another. For example, Moses taught that there was only one God; Krishna believed in many gods; and Buddha was agnostic. Logically, they can all be wrong but they can't all be right.

Furthermore, the road of religion leads steeply uphill, while the road of Christianity descends downward. Put another way, Religion is fallen humanity's attempt to reach up and become acceptable to God through what we *do*; Christianity, on the other hand, is a divine gift based on what Christ has *done*. He lived the perfect life that we

*It is incorrect
and illogical to maintain
that all religions
lead to God.*

could never live and offers us his perfection as an absolutely free gift.

Finally, Jesus taught that there was only one way to God. "I am *the way* and *the truth* and *the life*," said Jesus, "No one comes to the Father except through me" (John 14: 6, emphasis added). Moreover, Jesus validated his claim through the immutable fact of his resurrection. The opinions of all other religious leaders are equally valid in that they are equally worthless. They died and are still dead. Only Jesus had the power to lay down his life and to take it up again. Thus, his opinion is infinitely more valid than theirs.

For further study, see John MacArthur, *Why One Way? Defending an Exclusive Claim in an Inclusive World* (Nashville: W Publishing Group, 2002); and Ronald Nash, *Is Jesus the Only Savior?* (Grand Rapids: Zondervan, 1994).

ACTS 4:12

"Salvation is found in no one else,
for there is no other name under heaven given to men
by which we must be saved."

46

WHAT HAPPENS TO A PERSON
WHO HAS NEVER HEARD OF JESUS?

One of the most frequently asked questions on the *Bible Answer Man* broadcast is "What happens to those who have never heard of Jesus?" Will God condemn people to hell for not believing in someone they have never heard of?

First, people are not condemned to hell for not believing in Jesus. Rather they are *already* condemned because of their *sin*. Thus, the real question is not how can God send someone to hell, but how can God condescend to save any one of us?

Furthermore, if ignorance were a ticket to heaven, the greatest evangelistic enterprise would not be a Billy Graham crusade but a concerted cover-up campaign. Such a campaign would focus on ending evangelism, burning Bibles, and closing churches. Soon no one will have heard of Christ and everyone will be on their way to heaven.

Finally, it should be emphasized that everyone has the light of both creation and conscience. God is not capricious! If we respond to the light we have,

God will give us more light. In the words of the apostle Paul: "From one man he made every nation of men, that they should inhabit the whole earth; and he determined the times set for them and the exact places where they should live. God did this so that men would seek him and perhaps reach out for him and find him, though he is not far from each one of us" (Acts 17:26–27).

For further study, see Ronald H. Nash, *Is Jesus the Only Savior?* (Grand Rapids: Zondervan, 1994). See also Hank Hanegraaff, "Is Jesus the Only Way," available at www.equip.org.

JOHN 14:6

"I am the way and the truth and the life.
No one comes to the Father except through me."

47

IS THERE EVIDENCE FOR LIFE AFTER DEATH?

A theists believe that death is the cessation of being. In their view, humans are merely bodies and brains. Though they reject metaphysical realities such as the soul *a priori* (prior to examination), there are convincing reasons to believe that humans have an immaterial aspect to their being that transcends the material and thus can continue to exist after death. Christian philosopher J. P. Moreland advances several sound arguments for the existence of the immaterial soul.

First, from the perspective of logic, we can demonstrate that *the mind is not identical to the brain* by proving that the mind and brain have different properties. As Moreland explains: "the subjective texture of our conscious mental experiences—the feeling of pain, the experience of sound, the awareness of color—is different from anything that is simply physical. If the world were only made of matter, these subjective aspects of consciousness would not exist. But they *do* exist! So there must be more to the world than matter." An obvious example is color. A moment's reflection is enough to convince thinking people everywhere that the experience of color involves more than a mere wavelength of light.

Furthermore, from a legal perspective, if human beings were merely material, they could not be held accountable this year for a crime committed last year, because physical identity changes over time. Every day we lose multiplied millions of microscopic particles—in fact, every seven years, virtually every part of our material anatomy changes, apart from aspects of our neurological system. Therefore, from a purely material perspective, the person who previously committed a crime is presently not the same person. A criminal who attempts to use this line of reasoning as a defense would not get very far. Legally and intuitively, we recognize a *sameness of soul* that establishes personal identity over time.

Finally, libertarian freedom (freedom of the will) presupposes that we are more than mere material robots. If I am merely material, my choices are merely a function of such factors as genetic makeup and brain chemistry. Therefore, my decisions are not free; they are fatalistically determined. The implications of such a notion are profound. In a worldview that embraces fatalistic determinism, I cannot be held morally accountable for my actions, because reward and punishment make sense only if we have freedom of the will.

While the logical, legal, and libertarian freedom arguments are convincing in and of themselves, there is an even more powerful and persuasive argument demonstrating the reality of life beyond the grave. That argument flows from the resurrection of Jesus Christ. The best minds of ancient and modern times have demonstrated beyond a shadow of doubt that Christ's physical trauma was fatal; that the empty tomb is one of the best-attested facts of ancient history; that Christ's followers experienced on several occasions tangible post-resurrection appearances of Christ; and that within weeks of the resurrection, not just one, but an entire community of at least ten thousand Jews experienced such an incredible transformation that they willingly gave up sociological and theological traditions that had given them their national identity.

Through the resurrection, Christ not only demonstrated that he does not stand in a line of peers with Abraham, Buddha, or Confucius but also provided compelling evidence for life after death.

"I am the resurrection and the life.
He who believes in me will live,
even though he dies; and whoever lives
and believes in me will never die."

—JOHN 11:25-26

For further study, see Gary R. Habermas and J. P. Moreland, *Beyond Death: Exploring the Evidence for Immortality* (Wheaton, Ill.: Crossway Books, 1998).

"Do not be afraid of those who kill the body but cannot kill the soul. Rather, be afraid of the One who can destroy both soul and body in hell."

WHY DOES GOD ALLOW BAD THINGS
TO HAPPEN TO GOOD PEOPLE?

his is perhaps the most common question Christian celebrities are asked to answer on shows such as *Larry King Live*. At first blush, it may seem as though there are as many responses as there are religions. In reality, however, there are only three basic answers, namely pantheism, philosophical naturalism, and theism. *Pantheism* denies the existence of good and evil because in this view god is all and all is god. *Philosophical naturalism* (the worldview undergirding evolutionism) supposes that everything is a function of random processes, thus there is no such thing as good and evil. *Theism* alone has a relevant response—and only *Christian* theism can answer the question satisfactorily.

First, Christian theism acknowledges that God created the *potential* for evil because God created humans with freedom of choice. We choose to love or hate, to do good or evil. The record of history bears eloquent testimony to the fact that humans of their own free will have actualized the reality of evil through such choices.

Furthermore, without choice, love is meaningless. God is neither a cosmic rapist who forces his love on people, nor a cosmic puppeteer who forces people to love him. Instead, God, the personification of love, grants us the freedom of choice. Without such freedom, we would be little more than preprogrammed robots.

Finally, the fact that God created the potential for evil by granting us freedom of choice ultimately will lead to the best of all possible worlds—a world in which "there will be no more death or mourning or crying or pain" (Revelation 21:4). Those who choose Christ will be redeemed from evil by his goodness and will forever be able *not* to sin.

For further study, see Joni Eareckson Tada and Steven Estes, *When God Weeps* (Grand Rapids: Zondervan, 1997); Lee Strobel, *The Case for Faith* (Grand Rapids: Zondervan, 2000), chapter one.

ROMANS 8:28
"We know that in all things God works
for the good of those who love him, who have been
called according to his purpose."

49

IF CHRISTIANITY IS TRUE, WHY ARE SO MANY ATROCITIES COMMITTED IN THE NAME OF CHRIST?

his is a classic smokescreen question often asked to avoid having to grapple with the evidence for authentic Christianity. At best, it involves a hasty generalization. At worst, it's a way of "poisoning the well."

To begin with, this question was anticipated by Christ, who long ago proclaimed that his followers would be recognized by the way they lived their lives (John 15:8). Thus to classify as Christian those who are responsible for instigating atrocities, is to beg the question of who Christ's disciples are to begin with. As Jesus pointed out not everyone who calls him "Lord" is the real deal (Matthew 7:21–23).

Furthermore, this question implies that Christianity must be false on the basis that atrocities have been committed in Christ's name. There is no reason, however, why we can't turn the argument around and claim that Christianity must be true

*The validity of Christianity
does not rest on sinful men
but rather on the perfection of
Jesus Christ alone.*

because so much good has been done in the name of Christ. Think of the countless hospitals, schools, universities, and relief programs that have been instituted as a direct result of people who have the sacred name of Christ upon their lips.

Finally, those who use this argument fail to realize that the validity of Christianity does not rest on sinful men but rather on the perfection of Jesus Christ alone (Hebrews 7:26; 1 Peter 2:22). Moreover, the fact that professing Christians commit sins only serves to prove the premise of Christianity—namely, "all have sinned and fall short of the glory of God" (Romans 3:23); thus all are in need of a Savior (1 John 3:4–5).

For further study, see R. C. Sproul, *Reason to Believe* (Grand Rapids: Zondervan, 1982); Lee Strobel, *The Case for Faith* (Grand Rapids: Zondervan, 2000), chapters 4 and 7.

MATTHEW 7:21–23

"Not everyone who says to me, 'Lord, Lord,' will enter the kingdom of heaven, but only he who does the will of my Father who is in heaven. Many will say to me on that day, 'Lord, Lord, did we not prophesy in your name, and in your name drive out demons and perform many miracles?' Then I will tell them plainly, 'I never knew you. Away from me you evildoers!'"

This grace was given us

in Christ Jesus before the beginning

of time, but it has now been

revealed through the appearing of our

Savior, Christ Jesus, who has

destroyed death and has brought life

and immortality to

light through the gospel.

—2 TIMOTHY 1:9–10

50

CAN GOD CREATE A ROCK SO HEAVY
THAT HE CANNOT MOVE IT?

This question is a classic straw man that has most Christians looking like the proverbial deer in the headlights. At best, it challenges God's omnipotence. At worst, it undermines his existence.

First, there is a problem with the premise of the question. While it is true that God can do anything that is consistent with His nature, it is absurd to suggest that he can do everything. God cannot lie (Hebrews 6:18); he cannot be tempted (James 1:13); and he cannot cease to exist (Psalm 102:25–27).

It is crucial that we learn to question the question rather than assuming the question is valid.

Furthermore, just as it is impossible to make a one-sided triangle, so it is impossible to make a rock too heavy to be moved. What an all-powerful God can create he can obviously move. Put another way, God can do everything that is logically possible.

Finally, we should note that a wide variety of similar questions are raised to undermine the Christian view of God. Thus, it is crucial that we learn to question the question rather than assuming the question is valid.

For further study, see Norman L. Geisler, *Baker Encyclopedia of Christian Apologetics* (Grand Rapids: Baker Books, 1999), 553–554; see also 283–288. See also Hank Hanegraaff, "Indwelling of the Holy Spirit," available at www.equip.org.

PROVERBS 26:4–5
"Do not answer a fool according to his folly,
or you will be like him yourself.
Answer a fool according to his folly,
or he will be wise in his own eyes."

51

WHAT DOES IT MEAN TO SAY
THAT GOD IS OMNIPRESENT?

he Bible clearly portrays God's omnipresence. But, what exactly does that mean? Is God dispersed throughout the universe? Or does omnipresence refer to God's nearness to all of creation all of the time?

First, when Scripture speaks of God as omnipresent or present everywhere (Psalm 139), it is not communicating that he is physically distributed throughout the universe, but that he is simultaneously present (with all his fullness) to every part of creation. Thus, Scripture communicates God's creative and sustaining relationship to the cosmos rather than his physical location in the cosmos.

Furthermore, to speak of God's omnipresence in terms of his physical location in the world rather than his relationship to the world has more in common with the panentheism of heretical process theology (currently popular in liberal circles) than with classical Christian theism. Panentheism holds that God is intrinsically "in" the world (like a hand in a glove), while classical theism holds that God properly exists outside of time and space (Isaiah 57:15).

Finally, the danger of speaking about God in locational terms is that it logically implies that he is by nature a material being. The apostle John clearly communicates that "God is Spirit, and his worshipers must worship in spirit and in truth" (John 4:24).

For further study, see Gordon R. Lewis, "Attributes of God," in Walter A. Elwell, ed., *Evangelical Dictionary of Theology*, 2nd edition (Grand Rapids: Baker Academic, 2001), 492–499.

PSALM 139:7–10
"Where can I go from your Spirit?
Where can I flee from your presence?
If I go up to the heavens, you are there;
if I make my bed in the depths, you are there.
If I rise on the wings of the dawn,
if I settle on the far side of the sea,
even there your hand will guide me,
your right hand will hold me fast."

IS THE TRINITY BIBLICAL?

hile it has become increasingly popular to suggest that the doctrine of the Trinity is derived from pagan sources, in reality, this Christian essential is thoroughly biblical. The word "Trinity"—like "incarnation"— is not found in Scripture; however, it aptly codifies what God has condescended to reveal to us about his nature and being. In short, the Trinitarian platform contains three planks: (1) there is but one God; (2) the Father is God, the Son is God, and the Holy Spirit is God; (3) Father, Son and Holy Spirit are eternally distinct.

The first plank underscores that there is only one God. Christianity is not polytheistic but fiercely monotheistic. "You are my witnesses, declares the LORD, and my servant whom I have chosen, so that you may know and believe me and understand that I am he. *Before me no god was formed, nor will there be one after me*" (Isaiah 43:10, emphasis added).

The second plank emphasizes that in hundreds of Scripture passages the Father, Son, and Holy Spirit are declared to be fully and completely God. As a case in point, the Apostle Paul says that, "there is but one God, the Father" (1 Corinthians 8:6). The Father, speaking of the Son, says, "Your throne, O God, will last forever and forever" (Hebrews 1:8). And when Ananias "lied to the Holy Spirit," Peter points out that he had "not lied to men but to God" (Acts 5:3–4).

The third plank of the Trinitarian platform asserts that the Father, Son, and Holy Spirit are eternally distinct. Scripture clearly portrays subject/object relationships between Father, Son, and Holy Spirit. For example, the Father and Son love one another, speak to each other (John 17:1–26), and together send the Holy Spirit (John 15:26). Additionally, Jesus proclaims that he and the Father are two distinct witnesses and two distinct judges (John 8:14–18). If Jesus were himself the Father, his argument would not only have been irrelevant but it would have been fatally flawed; and if such were the case, he could not have been fully God.

It is important to note that when Trinitarians speak of one God they are referring to the nature or essence of God. Moreover, when they speak of persons they are referring to personal self-distinctions within the Godhead. Put another way, we believe in one *What* and three *Who's*.

For further study, see James R. White, *The Forgotten Trinity* (Minneapolis: Bethany House, 2001).

DEUTERONOMY 6:4

"Hear, O Israel: The LORD our God,
the LORD is one."

MATTHEW 28:19

"Therefore go and make disciples of all nations,
baptizing them in the name of the Father and of the
Son and of the Holy Spirit."

DOES THE BIBLE CLAIM JESUS IS GOD?

any biblical texts can be used to demonstrate that Jesus is God. Three, however, stand out above the rest. Not only are they clear and convincing, but their "addresses" are easy to remember as well—John *1*, Colossians *1*, and Hebrews *1*.

First, is *John 1*: "In the beginning was the Word, and the Word was with God, *and the Word was God*" (v.1). Here Jesus is not only in existence before the world began but is differentiated from the Father and explicitly called God, indicating that he shares the same nature as his Father.

Furthermore, *Colossians 1* informs us that *"all things were created by him"* (v. 16); he is *"before all things"* (v. 17); and *"God was pleased to have all his fullness dwell in him"* (v. 19). Only deity has the prerogative of creation, preexists all things, and personifies the full essence and nature of God.

Finally, *Hebrews 1* overtly tells us that according to God the Father himself—Jesus *is* God: *"But about the Son he* [the Father] *says, 'Your throne, O God, will last for ever and ever'"* (v. 8). Not only is the entirety of Hebrews 1 devoted to demonstrating the absolute deity of Jesus but in verses 10–12 the inspired writer quotes a passage in Psalm 102 referring to Yahweh and directly applies it to Christ. In doing so, the Scripture specifically declares Jesus ontologically equal with Israel's God.

Many similar texts could be adduced. For example, in *Revelation 1* the Lord God says, "I am the Alpha and the Omega, who is, and who was, and who is to come, the Almighty" (v. 8). In the last chapter of Revelation, Jesus applies these self same words— "Alpha and Omega"—to himself! Additionally, in *2 Peter 1* Jesus is referred to as "our God and Savior Jesus Christ" (v. 1). In these passages and a host of others, the Bible explicitly claims that Jesus *is* God.

For further study, see Hank Hanegraaff, *Resurrection* (Nashville: Word Publishing, 2000).

TITUS 2:13

"We wait for the blessed hope—the glorious appearing of our great God and Savior, Jesus Christ."

DID JESUS CLAIM TO BE GOD?

hen Jesus came to Caesarea Philippi, he asked his disciples the mother of all questions, *"Who do you say that I am?"* (Matthew 16:15, Mark 8:29, Luke 9:20). Mormons answer this question by saying that Jesus is the spirit brother of Lucifer; Jehovah's Witnesses answer by saying that Jesus is the archangel Michael; New Agers say Jesus is an avatar or enlightened messenger. Jesus, however, answered by claiming that he was God.

First, Jesus claimed to be the unique Son of God. As a result, the Jewish leaders tried to kill him because in "calling God His own Father, [Jesus was] making himself equal with God" (John 5:18). In John 8:58 Jesus went so far as to use the very words by which God revealed himself to Moses from the burning bush (Exodus 3:14). To the Jews this was the epitome of blasphemy for they knew that in doing so Jesus was clearly claiming to be God. On yet another occasion, Jesus explicitly told the Jews: "'I and the Father are one.' Again the Jews picked up stones to stone him, but Jesus said to them, 'I have shown you many great miracles from the Father. For which of these do you stone me?' 'We are not stoning you for any of these,' replied the Jews, 'but for blasphemy, because you, a mere man, claim to be God'" (John 10:30–33).

Furthermore, Jesus made an unmistakable claim to deity before the Chief Priests and the whole Sanhedrin. Caiaphas the High Priest asked him: "'Are you the Christ, the Son of the Blessed One?' 'I am,' said Jesus. 'And you will see the Son of Man sitting at the right hand of the Mighty One and coming on the clouds of heaven'" (Mark 14:61–62). A biblically illiterate person might well have missed the import of Jesus' words. Caiaphas and the Council, however, did not. They knew that in saying he was "the *Son of Man*" who would come "*on the clouds of heaven*" he was making an overt reference to the *Son of Man* in Daniel's prophecy (Daniel 7:13–14). And in doing so, he was not only claiming to be the preexistent Sovereign of the Universe but prophesying that he would vindicate his claim by judging the very court that was now condemning him. Moreover, by combining Daniel's prophecy with David's proclamation in Psalm 110, Jesus was claiming that he would sit upon the throne of Israel's God and share God's very glory. To students of the Old Testament this was the height of "blasphemy," thus "they all condemned him as worthy of death" (Mark 14:64).

Finally, Jesus claimed to possess the very attributes of God. For example, he claimed *omniscience* by telling Peter, "this very night, before the rooster crows, you will disown me three times" (Matthew 26:34); declared *omnipotence* by not only resurrecting Lazarus (John 11:43) but by raising himself from the dead (see John 2:19); and professed *omnipresence* by promising he would be with his disciples "to the very end of the age" (Matthew 28:20). Not only so, but Jesus said to the paralytic in Luke 5:20, "Friend, your sins are forgiven." In doing so, he claimed a prerogative reserved for God alone. In addition, when Thomas worshiped Jesus saying "My Lord and my God!" (John 20:28), Jesus responded with commendation rather than condemnation.

For further study, see Millard J. Erickson, *The Word Became Flesh: A Contemporary Incarnational Christology* (Grand Rapids: Baker Book House, 1996).

REVELATION 1:17–18
"I am the First and the Last. I am the Living One; I was dead, and behold I am alive for ever and ever!"

WHAT CREDENTIALS BACK UP
JESUS' CLAIM TO DEITY?

esus not only claimed to be God but also provided many convincing proofs that he indeed was divine.

First, Jesus demonstrated that he was God in human flesh by manifesting the credential of sinlessness. While the Qur'an exhorts Muhammad to seek forgiveness for his sins, the Bible exonerates Messiah saying Jesus "had no sin" (2 Corinthians 5:21). And this is not a singular statement. John declares, "and in him is no sin" (1 John 3:5), and Peter says Jesus "committed no sin, and no deceit was found in his mouth" (1 Peter 2:22). Jesus himself went so far as to challenge his antagonists asking, "Can any of you prove me guilty of sin?" (John 8:46)

Furthermore, Jesus demonstrated supernatural authority over sickness, the forces of nature, fallen angels, and even death itself. *Matthew 4* records that Jesus went throughout Galilee teaching, preaching "and healing every disease and sickness among the people" (v.23). *Mark 4* documents Jesus rebuking the wind and the waves saying, "Quiet! Be still!"

(v.39). In *Luke 4* Jesus encounters a man possessed by an evil spirit and commands the demon to "Come out of him!" (v.35). And in *John 4*, Jesus tells a royal official whose son was close to death, "Your son will live" (v.50). In fact, the four Gospels record how Jesus demonstrated ultimate power over death through the immutable fact of his resurrection.

Finally, the credentials of Christ's deity are seen in the lives of countless men, women, and children. Each day, people of every tongue and tribe and nation experience the resurrected Christ by repenting of their sins and receiving Jesus as Lord and Savior of their lives. Thus, they not only come to know about Christ evidentially, but experientially Christ becomes more real to them than the very flesh upon their bones.

For further study, see William Lane Craig, *Reasonable Faith: Christian Truth and Apologetics*, rev. ed. (Wheaton, Ill.: Crossway Books, 1994), chapters 7 and 8.

MATTHEW 11:2–5

"When John heard in prison what Christ was doing, he sent his disciples to ask him, 'Are you the one who was to come, or should we expect someone else?' Jesus replied, 'Go back and report to John what you hear and see; The blind receive sight, the lame walk, those who have leprosy are cured, the deaf hear, the dead are raised, and the good news is preached to the poor.'"

Have mercy on me, O God,
according to your unfailing love;
according to your great compassion
blot out my transgressions.
Wash away all my iniquity
and cleanse me from my sin.

For I know my transgressions,
and my sin is always before me.
Against you, you only, have I sinned
and done what is evil in your sight,
so that you are proved right when you speak
and justified when you judge.
Surely I was sinful at birth,
sinful from the time my mother conceived me.
Surely you desire truth in the inner parts;
you teach me wisdom in the inmost place.

Cleanse me with hyssop, and I will be clean;
wash me, and I will be whiter than snow.
Let me hear joy and gladness;
let the bones you have crushed rejoice.
Hide your face from my sins
and blot out all my iniquity.

Create in me a pure heart, O God,
and renew a steadfast spirit within me.
Do not cast me from your presence
or take your Holy Spirit from me.
Restore to me the joy of your salvation
and grant me a willing spirit, to sustain me.

Then I will teach transgressors your ways,
and sinners will turn back to you.
Save me from bloodguilt, O God,
the God who saves me,
and my tongue will sing of your righteousness.
O Lord, open my lips,
and my mouth will declare your praise.
You do not delight in sacrifice, or I would
bring it;
you do not take pleasure in burnt offerings.
The sacrifices of God are a broken spirit;
a broken and contrite heart,
O God, you will not despise.

In your good pleasure make Zion prosper;
build up the walls of Jerusalem.
Then there will be righteous sacrifices,
whole burnt offerings to delight you;
then bulls will be offered on your altar.

HOW CAN WE BE SURE
ABOUT THE RESURRECTION OF CHRIST?

I f devotees of the kingdom of the cults, adherents of world religions, or liberal scholars are correct, the biblical account of the resurrection of Christ is fiction, fantasy, or a gargantuan fraud. If, on the other hand, Christianity is factually reliable, his resurrection is the greatest feat in human history. No middle ground exists. The resurrection is history or hoax, miracle or myth, fact or fantasy.

First, liberal and conservative scholars alike agree that the body of Jesus was buried in the private tomb of Joseph of Arimathea. As a member of the Jewish court that condemned Jesus, Joseph of Arimathea is unlikely to be Christian fiction (Mark 15:43); Jesus' burial in the tomb of Joseph of Arimathea is substantiated by Mark's gospel (15:46) and is, therefore, far too early to have been the subject of legendary corruption; the earliest Jewish response to the resurrection of Christ presupposes the empty tomb (Matthew 28:11–13); and in the centuries following the resurrection, the fact of the empty tomb was forwarded by Jesus' friends and foes alike.

Additionally, when you understand the role of women in first-century Jewish society, what is extraordinary is that this empty tomb story would feature females as the discoverers of the empty tomb. The fact that women are the first witnesses to the empty tomb is most plausibly explained by the reality that—like it or not—they were the discoverers of the empty tomb. This shows that the gospel writers faithfully recorded what happened, even if it was embarrassing. In short, early Christianity could not have survived an identifiable tomb containing the corpse of Christ.

Furthermore, Jesus gave his disciples many convincing proofs that he had risen from the dead. Paul, for example, points out that Christ "appeared to more than five hundred of the brothers at the same time, most of whom are still living, though some have fallen asleep" (1 Corinthians 15:6). It would have been one thing to attribute these supernatural experiences to people who had already died. It was quite another to attribute them to multitudes who were still alive. As the famed New Testament scholar of Cambridge University C. H.

Dodd points out, "There can hardly be any purpose in mentioning the fact that most of the five hundred are still alive, unless Paul is saying in effect, 'The witnesses are there to be questioned.'"

Finally, what happened as a result of the resurrection is unprecedented in human history. In the span of a few hundred years, a small band of seemingly insignificant believers succeeded in turning an entire empire upside down. While it is conceivable that they would have faced torture, vilification, and even cruel deaths for what they fervently believed to be true, it is inconceivable that they would have been willing to die for what they knew to be a lie. As Dr. Simon Greenleaf, the famous Royall Professor of Law at Harvard put it: "If it were morally possible for them to have been deceived in this matter, every human motive operated to lead them to discover and avow their error . . . If then their testimony was not true, there was no possible motive for this fabrication."

No middle ground exists.
The resurrection is history or hoax,
miracle or myth, fact or fantasy.

For further study, see Hank Hanegraaff, *The Third Day* (Nashville: W Publishing Group, 2003); Lee Strobel, *The Case for Christ* (Zondervan, 1999); and see especially, William Lane Craig, *Reasonable Faith* (Crossway Books, 1996), chapter 8.

1 CORINTHIANS 15:13–20

"If there is no resurrection of the dead, then not even Christ has been raised. And if Christ has not been raised, our preaching is useless and so is your faith. More than that, we are then found to be false witnesses about God, for we have testified about God that he raised Christ from the dead. But he did not raise him if in fact the dead are not raised. For if the dead are not raised, then Christ has not been raised either. And if Christ has not been raised, your faith is futile; you are still in your sins. Then those also who have fallen asleep in Christ are lost. If only for this life we have hope in Christ, we are to be pitied more than all men. But Christ has indeed been raised from the dead, the firstfruits of those who have fallen asleep."

DO THE GOSPEL ACCOUNTS
CONTRADICT ONE ANOTHER?

uring a prime-time television special titled *The Search for Jesus*, Peter Jennings asserted that according to some scholars, "the New Testament has four different and sometimes contradictory versions of Jesus' life." The Jesus Seminar scholars Jennings referenced, however, are famous for an idiosyncratic brand of fundamentalism that supplants reason and evidential substance with rhetoric and emotional stereotypes. They have made a virtual art form out of exploiting "discrepancies" in the secondary details of the gospels.

One of the most frequently cited alleged contradictions involves the female discoverers of the empty tomb. According to Matthew, the discoverers were Mary Magdalene and another Mary (28:1); Mark says they were Mary Magdalene, Mary the mother of James, and Salome (16:1); Luke claims Mary Magdalene, Joanna, Mary the mother of James, and others (24:10); and John focuses solely on Mary Magdalene (20:18).

In providing a defensible argument against such dogmatic assertions, it is first helpful to point out that the gospels are *complimentary* rather than *contradictory*. If John, in the example cited above, had stipulated that Mary Magdalene was the *only* female to discover the empty tomb while the other gospels claimed that more than one woman was involved, we would be faced with an obvious contradiction. Instead, the complimentary details provided by the four gospel writers simply serve to flesh out the rest of the story.

Furthermore, credible scholars look for a reliable *core* set of facts in order to validate historical accounts. In this case, liberal and conservative scholars alike agree that the body of Jesus was buried in the tomb of Joseph of Arimathea. As a member of the Jewish court that convicted Jesus, Joseph is unlikely to be Christian fiction. Additionally, when we consider the role of women in first-century Jewish society, what is remarkable is that the empty tomb accounts would feature females as heroes of the story. This demonstrates that the gospel writers factually recorded what happened even if it was culturally embarrassing.

Finally, if each of the gospel writers presented secondary details in exactly the same manner, critics would dismiss their accounts on the basis of *collusion*. Instead, the Gospels provide unique yet mutually consistent perspectives on the events surrounding the empty tomb.

The principles above not only resolve the circumstances in the case at hand but all supposed contradictions highlighted by Peter Jennings in *The Search for Jesus*. We can safely conclude that far from being contradictory, the gospel accounts are clearly *complimentary*; a consensus of credible scholarship considers the *core* set of facts presented by the gospel writers to be authentic and reliable; and the unique perspectives provided by Matthew, Mark, Luke, and John preclude the possibility of *collusion*.

For further study concerning alleged contradictions in the Bible, see Gleason L. Archer, *New International Encyclopedia of Bible Difficulties* (Grand Rapids: Zondervan, 1982); concerning evidences for Christ's resurrection, see Hank Hanegraaff, *The Third Day* (Nashville: W Publishing Group, 2003). Also see Hank Hanegraaff, "The Search for Jesus Hoax," available at www.equip.org.

LUKE 1:1–4

"Many have undertaken to draw up an account of the things that have been fulfilled among us, just as they were handed down to us by those who from the first were eyewitnesses and servants of the word.

Therefore, since I myself have investigated everything from the beginning, it seemed good also to me to write an orderly account for you, most excellent Theophilus, so that you may know the certainty of the things you have been taught."

What Does It Mean to Say that Jesus Ascended into Heaven?

ver the years, I have heard more than one skeptic ridicule the notion that Jesus ascended into heaven before the very eyes of his disciples. In their view, even if Jesus were traveling at the speed of light he would not yet have escaped the confines of our universe. Not only that but he must surely be struggling with oxygen deprivation by now.

In response, let me first point out that to say Jesus ascended into heaven does not imply that he is traveling through space but rather that as the God-man he transcended time and space. Put another way, heaven is not located in time and space; it exists in another dimension.

Furthermore, the physical universe does not exhaust reality. It doesn't take a rocket scientist to understand that an effect such as the universe must have a cause greater than itself. This is self-evident not only to those who are philosophically sophisticated but to thinking people everywhere.

Thus, the notion that the creator of the universe transcended his universe should pose no problem.

Finally, I should note that God often uses physical examples to point to spiritual realities. Thus, the physical fact of Christ's ascension points to the greater truth that he is now glorified in the presence of God and that our glorification is divinely guaranteed as well.

For further study, see Peter Toon, *The Ascension of our Lord* (Nashville: Thomas Nelson, 1984).

ACTS 1:9–11

"After he said this, he was taken up
before their very eyes, and a cloud hid him from
their sight. They were looking intently up into the sky
as he was going, when suddenly two men
dressed in white stood beside them. 'Men of Galilee,'
they said, 'why do you stand here looking
into the sky? This same Jesus, who has been taken
from you into heaven, will come back
in the same way you have seen him go into heaven.'"

WAS CHRISTIANITY INFLUENCED
BY ANCIENT PAGAN MYSTERY RELIGIONS?

common refrain sung by those determined to demolish the biblical Jesus in the court of public opinion is that his life, death, burial, and resurrection are myths borrowed from ancient pagan mystery religions. Once reverberating primarily through the bastions of private academia, this refrain is now also commonly heard in public arenas.

The first prevailing myth widely circulated in this regard is that the similarities between Christianity and the mystery religions are striking. Purveyors of this mythology employ biblical language and then go to great lengths to concoct commonalities. Take, for example, the alleged similarities between Christianity and the cult of Isis. The god Osiris is supposedly murdered by his brother and buried in the Nile. The goddess Isis recovers the cadaver, only to lose it once again to her brother-in-law who cuts the body into fourteen pieces and scatters them around the world. After finding the parts, Isis "baptizes" each piece in the Nile River and Osiris is "resurrected."

The alleged similarities as well as the terminology used to communicate them are greatly exaggerated. Parallels between the "resurrection" of Osiris and the resurrection of Christ are an obvious stretch. And, sadly for the mysteries, this is as good as it gets. Other parallels typically cited by liberal scholars are even more far-fetched. Not only that but liberals have the chronology all wrong—most mysteries flourished long after the closing of the cannon of Scripture. Thus, it would be far more accurate to say that the mysteries were influenced by Christianity than the other way around.

Furthermore, the mystery religions reduced reality to a personal experience of enlightenment. Through secret ceremonies initiates experienced an esoteric transformation of consciousness that led them to believe that they were entering into a higher realm of reality. While followers of Christ were committed to essential Christian doctrines, devotees of the mysteries worked themselves into altered states of consciousness. They were committed to the notion that experience is a better teacher than words. In fact, the reason mystery religions are so named is that they directly involve secret esoteric practices and initiation rites. Far from being rooted in history and evidence, the mysteries reveled in hype and emotionalism.

Finally, the mystery religions were syncretistic in that adherents not only worshiped various pagan deities but also frequently embraced aspects of competing mystery religions while continuing to worship within their own cultic constructs. Not so with Christianity. Converts to Christ singularly placed their faith in the One who said, "I am the way and the truth and the life. No one comes to the Father except through me" (John 14:6).

For further study, see Ronald H. Nash, *The Gospel and the Greeks* (Richardson, Texas: Probe Books, 1992). See also Hank Hanegraaff, "Answering More Prime Time Fallacies," available at www.equip.org.

ACTS 17:29–31

"Therefore since we are God's offspring, we should not think that the divine being is like gold or silver or stone—an image made by man's design and skill. In the past God overlooked such ignorance, but now he commands all people everywhere to repent. For he has set a day when he will judge the world with justice by the man he has appointed. He has given proof of this to all men by raising him from the dead."

Is the Virgin Birth Miracle or Myth?

In an op-ed piece published by *The New York Times* (August 15, 2003), columnist Nicholas Kristof used the virgin conception of Jesus to shamelessly promote the Enlightenment's false dichotomy between faith and reason. In his words, "The faith in the Virgin Birth reflects the way American Christianity is becoming less intellectual and more mystical over time." Kristof ends his piece with the following patronization: "The heart is a wonderful organ, but so is the brain." Those who have a truly open mind, however, should resist rejecting the virgin birth *a priori* (prior to examination).

First, miracles are not only possible but they are necessary in order to make sense of the universe in which we live. According to modern science, the universe not only had a beginning, but it is unfathomably fine-tuned to support life. Not only so, but the origin of life, information in the genetic code, irreducible complexity in biological systems, and the phenomenon of the human mind pose intractable difficulties for merely natural explanations. Thus, reason forces us to look beyond the natural world to a supernatural Designer who periodically intervenes in the affairs of his created handiwork. In other words, if we are willing to believe that God created the heavens and the earth (Genesis 1:1), we should have no problem accepting the virgin birth.

Reason forces us to look beyond the natural world to a supernatural Designer who periodically intervenes in the affairs of his created handiwork.

Furthermore, we are compelled by reason and evidence to acknowledge that the Bible is divine rather than human in origin. Manuscript evidence, archaeology, predictive prophecy, and the science of statistical probability together provide a persuasive case for the reliability of Scripture. Thus, we may appeal legitimately to the Word of God as evidence for the virgin birth. Moreover, Christ, who demonstrated that he was God in human flesh through the undeniable fact of resurrection, pronounced the Scriptures infallible (John 10:35;

14:24–26; 15:26–27; 16:13; Hebrews 1:1–2). And if Christ concurs with the virgin birth, no one should have the temerity to contradict his claim.

Finally, while it is currently popular to suggest that the Gospel writers borrowed the virgin birth motif from pagan mythology, the facts say otherwise. Stories of gods having sexual intercourse with women—such as the sun-god Apollo becoming a snake and impregnating the mother of Augustus Caesar—hardly parallel the virgin birth account. Moreover, given the strict monotheistic worldview of New Testament authors it should stretch credulity beyond the breaking point to suppose they borrowed from pagan mythologies—especially myths extolling the sexual exploits of pagan gods!

It has become all too common for people to buy into what has been well described as "a unique brand of fundamentalism" that values rhetoric and emotional stereotypes over reason and evidential substance. Those who suppose that the virgin birth is mythological would be well served to carefully consider defensible arguments rather than uncritically swallowing dogmatic assertions.

For further study, see R. Douglas Geivett and Gary R. Habermas, eds., *In Defense of Miracles: A Comprehensive Case for God's Action in History* (Downers Grove, Ill.: InterVarsity Press, 1997).

MATTHEW 1:23

"'The virgin will be with child and will give birth to a son, and they will call him Immanuel'— which means, 'God with us.'"

In the sixth month, God sent the angel Gabriel to Nazareth, a town in Galilee, to a virgin pledged to be married to a man named Joseph, a descendant of David. The virgin's name was Mary. The angel went to her and said, "Greetings, you who are highly favored! The Lord is with you."

Mary was greatly troubled at his words and wondered what kind of greeting this might be. But the angel said to her, "Do not be afraid, Mary, you have found favor with God. You will be with child and give birth to a son, and you are to give him the name Jesus. He will be great and will be called the Son of the Most High. The Lord God will give him the throne of his father David, and he will reign over the house of Jacob forever; his kingdom will never end."

"How will this be," Mary asked the angel, "since I am a virgin?"

The angel answered, "The Holy Spirit will come upon you, and the power of the Most High will overshadow you. So the holy one to be born will be called the Son of God. Even Elizabeth your relative is going to have a child in her old age, and she who was said to be barren is in her sixth month. For nothing is impossible with God."

"I am the Lord's servant," Mary answered. "May it be to me as you have said." Then the angel left her.

—LUKE 1:26–38

WHY SHOULD I BELIEVE IN HELL?

he horrors of hell are such that they cause us to instinctively recoil in disbelief and doubt. Yet, there are compelling reasons that should cause us to erase such doubt from our minds.

First, Christ, the creator of the cosmos, clearly communicated hell's irrevocable reality. He spent more time talking about hell than he did about heaven. In the Sermon on the Mount alone (Matthew 5–7), he explicitly warned his followers about the dangers of hell a half dozen or more times. In the Olivet Discourse (Matthew 24–25), Christ repeatedly warned his followers of the judgment that is to come. And, in his famous story of the Rich Man and Lazarus (Luke 16), Christ graphically portrayed the finality of eternal torment in hell.

Furthermore, the concept of choice demands that we believe in hell. Without hell, there is no choice. And without choice, heaven would not be heaven; heaven would be hell. The righteous would inherit a counterfeit heaven, and the unrighteous would be incarcerated in heaven against their wills, which would be a torture worse than hell. Imagine spending a lifetime voluntarily distanced from God only to find yourself involuntarily dragged into his loving presence for all eternity; the alternative to hell is worse than hell itself in that humans made in the image of God would be stripped of freedom and forced to worship God against their will.

Finally, common sense dictates that there must be a hell. Without hell, the wrongs of Hitler's Holocaust will never be righted. Justice would be impugned if, after slaughtering six million Jews, Hitler merely died in the arms of his mistress with no eternal consequences. The ancients knew better than to think such a thing. David knew that for a time it might seem as though the wicked prosper in spite of their deeds, but in the end justice will be served.

Common sense also dictates that without a hell there is no need for a Savior. Little needs to be said about the absurdity of suggesting that the Creator should suffer more than the cumulative sufferings of all of mankind, if there were no hell to save us from. Without hell, there is no need for salvation. Without salvation, there is no need for a sacrifice. And without sacrifice, there is no need for a Savior. As much as we may wish to think that all will be saved, common sense precludes the possibility.

Christ spent
more time talking
about hell than he did
about heaven.

For further study, see Hank Hanegraaff, *Resurrection* (Nashville: Word Publishing, 2000), chapter seven.

Daniel 12:2

"Multitudes who sleep in the dust of the earth will awake: some to everlasting life, others to shame and everlasting contempt."

"There was a rich man who was dressed in purple and fine linen and lived in luxury every day. At his gate was laid a beggar named Lazarus, covered with sores and longing to eat what fell from the rich man's table. Even the dogs came and licked his sores.

"The time came when the beggar died and the angels carried him to Abraham's side. The rich man also died and was buried. In hell, where he was in torment, he looked up and saw Abraham far away, with Lazarus by his side. So he called to him, 'Father Abraham, have pity on me and send Lazarus to dip the tip of his finger in water and cool my tongue, because I am in agony in this fire.'

"But Abraham replied, 'Son, remember that in your lifetime you received your good things, while Lazarus received bad things, but now he is comforted here and you are in agony. And besides all this, between us and you a great chasm has been fixed, so that those who want to go from here to you cannot, nor can anyone cross over from there to us.'

"He answered, 'Then I beg you, father, send Lazarus to my father's house, for I have five brothers. Let him warn them, so that they will not also come to this place of torment.'

"Abraham replied, 'They have Moses and the Prophets; let them listen to them.'

"'No, father Abraham,' he said, 'but if someone from the dead goes to them, they will repent.'

"He said to him, 'If they do not listen to Moses and the Prophets, they will not be convinced even if someone rises from the dead.'"

—LUKE 16:19–31

IS ANNIHILATIONISM BIBLICAL?

ust as universalism is the rage in liberal Christianity, so too annihilation is gaining momentum in conservative Christian circles. The question of course is— is annihilationism biblical?

First, common sense dictates that a God of love and justice does not arbitrarily annihilate the crowning jewels of his creation. Far from rubbing us out, He graciously provides us the freedom to choose between redemption and rebellion. It would be a horrific evil to think that God would create people with freedom of choice and then annihilate them because of their choices.

Furthermore, common sense leads to the conclusion that nonexistence is not better than existence since nonexistence is nothing at all—as Norman Geisler aptly puts it, "to affirm that nothing can be better than something is a gigantic category mistake." It also is crucial to recognize that not all existence in hell is equal. We may safely conclude that

Annihilationism:
The belief that at death or some
time thereafter those who reject Christ
will simply cease to exist.

the torment of Hitler's hell will greatly exceed the torment experienced by a garden-variety pagan.

God is perfectly just, and each person who spurns his grace will suffer exactly what he deserves (Luke 12:47–48; Matthew 16:27; Colossians 3:25; Revelation 20:11–15; Proverbs 24:12).

Finally, humans are fashioned in the very image of God; therefore, to eliminate them would do violence to his nature. The alternative to annihilation is quarantine. And that is precisely what hell is.

For further study, see Robert A. Peterson, *Hell on Trial: The Case for Eternal Punishment* (Phillipsburg, New Jersey: Presbyterian and Reformed Press, 1995).

REVELATION 14:9–11

"If anyone worships the beast and his image and receives his mark on the forehead or on the hand, he, too, will drink of the wine of God's fury, which has been poured full strength into the cup of his wrath. He will be tormented with burning sulfur in the presence of the holy angels and of the Lamb. And the smoke of their torment rises for ever and ever. There is no rest day or night for those who worship the beast and his image, or for anyone who receives the mark of his name."

WHAT ABOUT PURGATORY?

Roman Catholicism teaches that believers incur debts that must inevitably be discharged in Purgatory "before the gates of heaven can be opened." While Purgatory is not equivalent to a second chance for unbelievers, it is nonetheless decidedly unbiblical.

First, the doctrine of Purgatory undermines the sufficiency of Christ's atonement on the cross. Scripture declares that Christ through "one sacrifice . . . has made perfect forever those who are being made holy" (Hebrews 10:14; see also Hebrews 1:3). Thus, we can rest assured that Christ received in his own body all the punishment we deserved, absolutely satisfying the justice of God on our behalf (Romans 3:25–26; 2 Corinthians 5:19, 21; 1 Peter 3:18; 1 John 2:2). When Jesus cried out from the cross, "It is finished!" (John 19:30) he was in effect saying, "The debt has been paid in full."

Furthermore, Roman Catholicism clearly undermines the seriousness of sin by forwarding the notion that there are venial sins that can be atoned for through temporal punishment in Purgatory. In reality, as the Bible makes clear, all our transgressions and iniquities are sins against a holy eternal God (Psalm 51:4). And as such, they rightly incur an eternal rather than a temporal debt (Ezekiel 18:4; Matthew 5–7; Romans 6:23; James 2:10).

Finally, while Purgatory was officially defined by the Council of Florence (1439) and officially defended by the Council of Trent in the late 16th century, nowhere is Purgatory officially depicted in the canon of Scripture. As *The New Catholic Encyclopedia* readily acknowledges, "the doctrine of Purgatory is not explicitly stated in the Bible." Thus, Catholicism is forced to appeal to the traditions of the fathers rather than the testimony of the Father—who through his Word has graciously provided salvation by grace alone, though faith alone, on account of Christ alone (Romans 4:2–8; 11:6; Ephesians 2:8–9).

For further study, see Norman L. Geisler and Ralph E. MacKenzie, *Roman Catholics and Evangelicals: Agreements and Differences* (Grand Rapids: Baker Books, 1995).

HEBREWS 10:14

"By one sacrifice he has made perfect
forever those who are being made holy."

IS THE ALLAH OF ISLAM
THE GOD OF THE BIBLE?

ong before Muhammad was born, Arabic
Christians already were referring to God as
Allah—and millions continue do so today.
The Allah of Islam, however, is definitely not the God
of the Bible. For while Muslims passionately defend
the unity of God they patently deny His triunity.
Thus, they recoil at the notion of God as Father,
reject the unique deity of Jesus Christ the Son, and
renounce the divine identity of the Holy Spirit.

First, while the Master taught his disciples to pray
"Our Father in heaven," devotees of Muhammad find
the very notion offensive. To their way of thinking,
calling God, "Father" and Jesus Christ, "Son" suggests
sexual procreation. According to the Qur'an, "It is not
befitting to (the majesty of) Allah that He should
beget a son" (Sura 19:35), Allah "begetteth not, nor is
he begotten"(Sura 112:3). The Bible however does not
use the term "begotten" with respect to the Father and
the Son in the sense of sexual reproduction but rather
in the sense of special relationship. Thus, when the

apostle John speaks of Jesus as "the only *begotten* of the Father" (John 1:14 NKJV, emphasis added), he is underscoring the unique deity of Christ. Likewise, when the Apostle Paul refers to Jesus as "the *firstborn* over all creation" (Colossians 1:15, emphasis added) he is emphasizing Christ's preeminence or prime position as the Creator of *all* things (Colossians 1:16–19). Christians are sons of God through adoption; Jesus is God the Son from all eternity.

Furthermore, Muslims dogmatically denounce the Christian declaration of Christ's unique deity as the unforgivable sin of *shirk*. As the Qur'an puts it, "God forgiveth not the sin of joining other gods with Him; but He forgiveth whom He pleaseth other sins than this" (Sura 4:116). While Muslims readily affirm the sinlessness of Christ, they adamantly deny His sacrifice upon the cross and subsequent resurrection. In doing so, they deny the singular historic fact which demonstrates that Jesus does not stand in a long line of peers from Abraham to Muhammad, but is God in human flesh. The Qur'anic phrase, "Allah raised him up" (Sura 4:158) is taken to mean that Jesus was supernaturally raptured rather than resurrected from the dead. In Islamic lore, God made someone look like Jesus, and this look-a-like was crucified in his place. In recent years, the myth that Judas was crucified in place of Jesus has been popularized in Muslim circles by a late medieval invention titled *The Gospel of Barnabas*. Against the weight of history and evidence the Qur'an exudes, "they killed him not, nor crucified him, but so it was made to appear to them" (Sura 4:157).

Finally, in addition to rejecting the divinity of Jesus, Islam also renounces the divine identity of the Holy Spirit. Far from being the third person of the Triune God who inspired the text of the Bible, Islam teaches that the Holy Spirit is the archangel Gabriel who dictated the Qur'an to Muhammad over a period of twenty-three years. Ironically, while the Holy Spirit who dictated the Qur'an is said to be the archangel Gabriel, Islam identifies the Holy Spirit promised by Jesus in John 14 as Muhammad. The Bible, however, roundly rejects such corruptions and misrepresentation. Biblically the Holy Spirit is neither an angel nor a mere mortal; rather he is the very God who redeems us from our sins and will one day resurrect us to life eternal (Acts 5:3–4; Romans 8:11).

For further study, see Timothy George, *Is the Father of Jesus the God of Muhammad?* (Grand Rapids: Zondervan, 2002).

1 JOHN 2:23
*"No one who denies the Son has the Father;
whoever acknowledges the Son has the Father also."*

Is the Qur'an Credible?

ccording to Islam, the Qur'an is not only credible; it is God's *only* uncorrupted revelation. Thus, according to Muslim scholars, if it is to be compared with anything in Christianity it is to be compared with Christ rather than the Bible. In truth, however, the Bible can be demonstrated to be divine rather than human in origin. The same cannot be said for the Qur'an. Moreover, unlike the Bible the Qur'an is replete with faulty ethics and factual errors.

First, unlike the Qur'an, the Bible is replete with prophecies that could not have been fulfilled through chance, good guessing, or deliberate deceit. Surprisingly, the predictive nature of many Bible passages was once a popular argument among liberals against the reliability of the Bible. Critics argued that various passages were written later than the biblical texts indicated because they recounted events that happened sometimes hundreds of years after they supposedly were written. They concluded that subsequent to the events, literary editors went back and "doctored" the original nonpredictive texts. But this is simply wrong. Careful research *affirms* the predictive accuracy of the Scriptures. Since Christ is the culminating theme of the Old Testament and the Living Word of the New Testament, it should not surprise us that prophecies regarding him outnumber all others. Many of these prophesies would have been impossible for Jesus to deliberately conspire to fulfill—such as his descent from Abraham, Isaac, and Jacob (Genesis 12:3; 17:19; Matthew 1:1–2; Acts 3:25); his birth in Bethlehem (Micah 5:2; Matthew 2:1–6); his crucifixion with criminals (Isaiah 53:12; Matthew 27:38; Luke 22:37); the piercing of his hands and feet on the cross (Psalm 22:16; John 20:25); the soldiers gambling for his clothes (Psalm 22:18; Matthew 27:35); the piercing of his side (Zechariah 12:10; John 19:34); the fact that his bones were not broken at his death (Psalm 34:20; John 19:33–37); and his burial among the rich (Isaiah 53:9; Matthew 27:57–60).

In sharp contrast, predictive prophecies demonstrating the divine origin of the Qur'an are conspicuous by their absence. While the Qur'an contains a number of self-fulfilling prophecies such as Muhammad's prediction that he would return to Mecca (Sura 48:27), this is very different from the kinds of prophecies outlined above. Other prophecies such as Muhammad's prediction that the Romans would defeat the Persians at Issus (Sura 30:2–4) are equally underwhelming. Unlike the biblical examples presented above this prophecy is not fulfilled in the far future and thus can be easily explained through good guessing or an accurate apprehension of prevailing military conditions.

Furthermore, the Qur'an is replete with questionable ethics—particularly when it comes to the equality of women. For example, in Sura 4:3 Muhammad allegedly received a revelation from God allowing men to "marry women of your choice, two, three, or four." Ironically, in Sura 33:50 Muhammad receives a divine sanction to marry "any believing woman who dedicates her soul to the Prophet if the Prophet wishes to wed her." Thus while other men were only permitted to marry up to four wives, Allah provided Muhammad with a divine exception for his marriage to at least twelve women—including Aishah, whom he married at the tender age of eleven (see the *Life of Muhammad* by Muhammad Husayn Haykal). Also troubling is the fact that the Qur'an allows men to "beat" (lightly) their wives in order that they might "return to obedience" (Sura 4:34). When we compare the personal morality of Muhammad in the Qur'an with that of Jesus in the Bible, the difference is remarkable. The Qur'an exorts Muhammad to ask "forgiveness for thy fault" (Sura 40:55). Conversely, Christ's ethics with regard to every aspect of life—including his treatment of women—was so unimpeachable that he could rightly ask: "Can any of you prove me guilty of sin?" (John 8:46, 2 Corinthians 5:21, 1 John 3:5)

Finally, unlike the Bible the Qur'an is riddled with factual errors. A classic case in point involves the Qur'an's denial of Christ's crucifixion. This denial chronicled in Sura 4:157 is explicit and emphatic: "They killed him not, nor crucified him, but so it was made to appear to them…for of a surety they killed him not." In reality, however, the fatal suffering of Jesus Christ as recounted in the New Testament is one of the most well established facts of ancient history. Even in today's modern age of scientific enlightenment, there is a virtual consensus among New Testament scholars, both conservative and liberal, that Jesus died on a Roman cross.

Recent archaeological discoveries not only dramatically corroborate the Bible's description of Roman crucifixion but authenticate the biblical details surrounding the trail that led to the fatal torment of Jesus Christ—including the Pilate Stone and the burial grounds of Caiaphas, the high priest who presided over the religious trials of Christ. These discoveries have been widely acclaimed as a compelling affirmation of biblical history. Not only so but the earliest Jewish response to the death and burial of Jesus Christ presuppose the reality of the empty tomb. Instead of denying that the tomb was empty, the antagonists of Christ accused his disciples of stealing the body.

One final point should be made. The Qur'anic denial of Christ's crucifixion has led to a host of other errors as well. From a Muslim perspective, Jesus was never crucified and, thus, never resurrected. Instead, in Islam, God made someone look like Jesus and the look-alike was mistakenly crucified in his place. The notion that Judas was made to look like Jesus has recently been popularized in Muslim circles by a late medieval invention titled *The Gospel of Barnabas*.

In short, the distance between the Muslim Qur'an and the Christian Scriptures is the distance of infinity. Not only does the prophetic prowess of the Bible elevate it far above the holy books of other religions, but as new archeological nuggets are uncovered the trustworthiness of Scripture as well as the unreliability of pretenders are further

Faulty ethics and factual errors demonstrate that the Qur'an is devoid of divine sanction. In sharp distinction, ethics and factual evidence demonstrate that the Bible is divine rather than human in origin.

highlighted. Faulty ethics and factual errors demonstrate that the Qur'an is devoid of divine sanction. In sharp distinction, ethics and factual evidence demonstrate that the Bible is divine rather than human in origin.

For further study, see Norman L. Geisler & Abdul Saleeb, *Answering Islam* (Grand Rapids: Baker Books, 2002).

HEBREWS 1:1–3

"In the past God spoke to our forefathers through the prophets at many times and in various ways, but in these last days he has spoken to us by his Son, whom he appointed heir of all things, and through whom he made the universe. The Son is the radiance of God's glory and the exact representation of his being, sustaining all things by his powerful word. After he had provided purification for sins, he sat down at the right hand of the Majesty in heaven."

WHAT IS A CULT?

Larry King asked me this very question after thirty-nine people took their lives in the largest mass suicide in U.S. history. He went on to ask whether Christianity might legitimately be referred to as a cult. As I explained on *Larry King Live* the word "cult" has various connotations.

First, a cult may be defined *sociologically*. From this perspective, a cult is a religious or semi-religious sect whose followers are controlled by strong leadership in virtually every dimension of their lives. Devotees characteristically display a displaced loyalty for the guru and the group and are galvanized together through physical and/or psychological intimidation tactics. This kind of cultist more often than not displays a "we/they" siege mentality and has been cut off from all former associations including their immediate families.

Furthermore, a cult may be defined *theologically*. In this sense a cult can be a pseudo-Christian organization that claims to be Christian but

*In dealing with cults
it is crucial to be
diligent in defining terms.*

compromises, confuses, or contradicts essential Christian doctrine. Such cults operate under the guise of Christianity but deviate from the orthodox teachings of the historic Christian faith as codified in the ancient ecumenical creeds. Typically, devotees become masters at taking texts out of context to develop pretexts for their theological perversions.

Finally, I should note that although the media-driven culture has given the term "cult" an exclusively pejorative connotation, denotatively the word "cult" can be broadly defined as a group of people centered around a religious belief structure. As such, Christianity might rightly be referred to as a cult of Old Testament Judaism. In fact, the Latin verb *cultus* from which we derive the word "cult" simply means to worship a deity. Thus, in dealing with cults it is crucial to be diligent in defining terms.

For further study, see Hank Hanegraaff, *Counterfeit Revival*, rev. ed. (Nashville: Word Publishing Group, 2001), part 5; and Ron Rhodes, *The Challenge of the Cults and New Religions* (Grand Rapids: Zondervan, 2001).

2 CORINTHIANS 11:3–4

"But I am afraid that just as Eve was deceived by the serpent's cunning, your minds may somehow be led astray from your sincere and pure devotion to

Christ. For if someone comes to you and preaches a Jesus other than the Jesus we preached, or if you receive a different spirit from the one you received, or a different gospel from the one you accepted, you put up with it easily enough."

ARE THERE APOSTLES
AND PROPHETS TODAY?

While it has become increasingly popular to believe in the restoration of "end-time" apostles and prophets, the Bible clearly does not support this notion.

First, to address this question we must first learn to scale the language barrier. In other words, the issue is not so much the words "prophet" or "apostle" but the meaning that is ascribed to these words. For example, *apostle* may be used in the sense of a church planter, a missionary, or a pastor of pastors. Likewise, *prophet* may be used in the sense of a leader who inspires the church with vision for its mission or who challenges the church to deeper commitment to Christ. However, the words "apostle" and "prophet" must not be used in a synonymous sense with the first-century apostle John or the Old Testament prophet Jeremiah. People whose authority cannot be questioned or who receive new doctrinal revelations simply do not exist today.

Furthermore, the Bible teaches that apostles and prophets were commissioned by God to be His personal spokesmen. Moreover, Ephesians 2:20 tells us that the church is "built on the foundation of the apostles and prophets, with Christ Jesus himself as the chief cornerstone." Clearly, then, those who claim to be that kind of apostle and prophet today have taken upon themselves authority that was not given to them by God.

Finally, the prophetic words of Scripture expose today's pretenders. Not only do they fail the biblical tests given in Deuteronomy 13 and 18, as well as Acts 1:21–22, but "they mouth empty, boastful words and, by appealing to the lustful desires of sinful human nature, they entice people who are just escaping from those who live in error. They promise freedom, while they themselves are slaves of depravity" (2 Peter 2:18–19).

For further study, see Hank Hanegraaff, *Counterfeit Revival: Looking for God in All the Wrong Places*, rev. ed. (Nashville: Word Publishing, 2001).

"'How can we know when a message has not been spoken by the LORD?' If what a prophet proclaims in the name of the LORD does not take place or come true, that is a message the LORD has not spoken. That prophet has spoken presumptuously. Do not be afraid of him."

ARE JEHOVAH'S WITNESSES CHRISTIAN?

Like Mormons, Jehovah's Witnesses believe that Christianity died with the last of the apostles. They believe Christianity was not resurrected until their founder, Charles Taze Russell, began organizing the Watchtower Society in the 1870s. In their view the cross is a pagan symbol adopted by an apostate church and salvation is impossible apart from the Watchtower. While the Witnesses on your doorstep consider themselves to be the only authentic expression of Christianity, the Society they serve compromises, confuses, or contradicts essential Christian doctrine.

First, the Watchtower Society compromises the nature of God. They teach their devotees that the Trinity is a "freakish-looking, three headed God" invented by Satan and that Jesus is merely a god. In Watchtower theology Jesus was created by God as the archangel Michael, during his earthly sojourn became merely human, and after his crucifixion was re-created an immaterial spirit creature. JW's also deny the physical resurrection of Jesus. According to

A host of doctrinal perversions keep Jehovah's Witnesses from rightly being considered Christian.

Russell, the body that hung on a torture stake either "dissolved into gasses" or is "preserved somewhere as the grand memorial of God's love."

Furthermore, while Christians believe all believers will spend eternity with Christ in "a new heaven and a new earth" (Revelation 21:1, 22:17) the Watchtower teaches that only 144,000 people will make it to heaven while the rest of the faithful will live apart from Christ on earth. Thus in Watchtower lore there is a "little flock" of 144,000 who get to go to heaven and a "great crowd" of others who are relegated to earth. The heavenly class are born again, receive the baptism of the Holy Spirit, and partake of communion; the earthly class do not. To substantiate the notion that heaven's door was closed irrevocably in 1935, JW's point to "flashes of prophetic light" received by Joseph F. Rutherford at a JW convention in Washington D.C. Other false "flashes of prophetic light" include Watchtower predictions of end-time cataclysms that were to occur in 1914 . . . 1918 . . . 1925 . . . 1975.

Finally, under the threat of being "disfellowshipped," Jehovah's Witnesses are barred from celebrating Christmas, birthdays, or holidays such as Thanksgiving and Good Friday. Even more troubling are Watchtower regulations regarding vaccinations, organ transplants, and blood transfusions. In 1931, JW's were instructed to refuse vaccinations—by 1952, this regulation was rescinded. In 1967, organ transplants were ruled a forbidden form of cannibalism—by 1980, this edict was erased. In 1909, the Watchtower produced a prohibition against blood transfusions. No doubt, this too will one day become a relic of the past. In the meantime, tens of thousands have not only been ravished spiritually by the Watchtower Society but have paid the ultimate physical price as well.

While Watchtower adherents are often willing to do more for a lie than Christians are willing to do for the truth, these and a host of other doctrinal perversions keep JW's from rightly being considered Christian.

For further study, see Ron Rhodes, *Reasoning from the Scriptures with the Jehovah's Witnesses* (Eugene, Ore.: Harvest House Publishers, 1993).

DEUTERONOMY 18:22

"If what a prophet proclaims in the name of the Lord does not take place or come true, that is a message the Lord has not spoken. That prophet has spoken presumptuously. Do not be afraid of him."

Is the New World Translation
of the Bible Credible?

ehovah's Witnesses claim that the *New World Translation* (*NWT*) is the "work of competent scholars." Conversely, they contend that other Bible translations are corrupted by religious traditions that are rooted in paganism. In reality, the *NWT* is the work of a Bible Translation Committee with no working knowledge of biblical languages. Their bias is so blatant that Dr. Bruce Metzger, professor of New Testament at Princeton, not only characterized the *NWT* as a "frightful mistranslation" but as "erroneous," "pernicious," and "reprehensible."

First, the *NWT* mistranslates the Greek Scriptures in order to expunge the deity of Jesus Christ. Against all credible scholarship, Jesus is downgraded from God to "*a*" god in John 1 and demoted from the Creator of all things to a mere creature who created all *other* things in Colossians 1. According to the translation committee of the Watchtower Society, Jesus was created by God as the

Greek scholars across the board
denounce the New World Translation
. . . "frightful mistranslation,"
"erroneous," "pernicious," and
"reprehensible."

archangel Michael, during his earthly sojourn was merely human, and after his crucifixion was re-created an immaterial spirit creature.

Furthermore, the Translation Committee has sought to conform the *NWT* to their religious traditions by replacing the *cross* of Christ with a *torture stake*. Matthew 10:38, for example, has been altered to read, "And whoever does not accept his *torture stake* and follow after me is not worthy of me." In Watchtower lore, the cross is a pagan symbol adopted by an apostate Christianity when Satan took control of the early church. Jehovah's Witnesses view wearing a cross as a blatant act of idolatry. Conversely, Christians wear crosses as a reminder of what was at once the most brutal and beautiful act in redemptive history.

Finally, the Watchtower Society claims that the Christian Scriptures have "been tampered with" in order to eliminate the name *Jehovah* from the text. In reality, it is the Translation Committee of the *NWT* that can rightly be accused of tampering. In well over two hundred cases the name Jehovah has been gratuitously inserted into the New Testament text. In passages such as Romans 10:13 this is done to obscure the unique deity of Christ. In other passages, it is done under the pretext that referring to God as

Lord rather than Jehovah is patently pagan. Ironically, in *The Kingdom Interlinear Translation of the Greek Scriptures*, Watchtower translators themselves fall into this "pagan" practice by translating the Greek word *kurios* as Lord even in cases where it specifically refers to the Father.

For these and a host of other reasons, Greek scholars across the board denounce the *NWT*. Dr. Julius Mantey, author of *A Manual Grammar of the Greek New Testament*, called the *NWT* a "shocking mistranslation," and Dr. William Barclay characterized the translators themselves as "intellectually dishonest."

For further study, see David A. Reed, *Answering Jehovah's Witnesses: Subject by Subject* (Grand Rapids: Baker Book House, 1996).

REVELATION 22:18–19

"I warn everyone who hears the words of the prophecy of this book: If anyone adds anything to them, God will add to him the plagues described in this book. And if anyone takes words away from this book of prophecy, God will take away from him his share in the tree of life and in the holy city, which are described in this book."
(SEE ALSO DEUTERONOMY 4:2)

IS MORMONISM CHRISTIAN?

The Church of Jesus Christ of Latter-day Saints was birthed in 1820 by an alleged vision in which two celestial personages appeared to Joseph Smith claiming *all* existing churches were wrong, *all* their creeds were an abomination, and *all* their professors were corrupt. According to these personages, Smith had been chosen to *restore*—not *reform*—a church that had disappeared from the face of the earth. The Mormon doctrines that evolved from this vision compromise, confuse, or contradict the nature of God, the authority of Scripture, and the way of salvation.

First, while Christians believe that God is spirit (John 4:24), Joseph Smith taught, "God Himself was once as we are now, and is an exalted man, and sits enthroned in yonder heavens!" Mormonism also holds to a plurality of gods and contends that "as man is, God once was; as God is, man may become." Additionally, the Latter-day Saints compromise the nature of the God-man, Jesus Christ. In Christianity, Jesus is the self-existent creator of all things

(Colossians 1:15–20). In Mormonism, he is the spirit brother of Lucifer who was conceived in heaven by a celestial Mother and came in flesh as the result of the Father having sex with the Virgin Mary.

Doctrinal perversions exclude
Mormonism from rightly being called Christian.

Furthermore, in sharp distinction to orthodox Christian theology, Mormons do not believe that the Bible is the *infallible* repository for redemptive revelation (2 Timothy 3:16). In their view, the *Book of Mormon* is "the most correct of any book on earth, and the keystone of our religion." Two further revelations complete the Mormon quad, namely *Doctrine and Covenants* and *The Pearl of Great Price*. *Doctrine and Covenants* is a compilation of divine revelations that includes the doctrine of polygamy. Not until threatened by the federal government did Mormon president Wilford Woodruff receive a revelation relegating polygamy to the afterlife. *The Pearl of Great Price* is no less troubling; this extra-biblical revelation was used by Mormonism to prevent African-Americans from entering the priesthood and from being exalted to godhood.

Finally, while Christians believe that they will stand before God dressed in the spotless robes of Christ's righteousness (Romans 3:21–22; Philippians 3:9), Mormons contend that they will appear before heavenly Father dressed in fig-leaf aprons holding good works in their hands. According to the Latter-day Saints, virtually everyone qualifies for heaven. Murderers, unrepentant whoremongers, and the world's vilest people make it into the *Telestial heaven*; lukewarm Mormons, religious people, and those who accept the Mormon gospel in the spirit world typically enter the *Terrestrial heaven*; and temple Mormons make it to the *Celestial heaven*. Only those who are sealed in secret temple rituals, however, will make it to the third level of the Celestial kingdom and become gods of their own planets.

These and many other doctrinal perversions exclude Mormonism from rightly being called Christian.

For further study, see Richard Abanes, *One Nation Under Gods* (New York: Four Walls Eight Windows, 2003).

ISAIAH 43:10

"You are my witnesses," declares the LORD,
"and my servant whom I have chosen,
so that you may know and believe me and understand
that I am he. Before me no god was formed,
nor will there be one after me."

Is the Book of Mormon Credible?

In 1823, the angel Moroni allegedly visited Mormon prophet Joseph Smith and divulged the location of some golden plates containing the "fullness of the everlasting gospel." These plates—abridged by Moroni and his father, Mormon, 1400 years earlier—were written in "reformed Egyptian hieroglyphics." Along with the plates, Smith found a pair of magical eyeglasses that he used to translate the cryptic writing into English. The result was a new revelation called the *Book of Mormon* and a new religion called *Mormonism*. How millions can take the *Book of Mormon* seriously is almost beyond comprehension.

First, while Smith referred to the *Book of Mormon* as "the most correct of any book on earth and the keystone of our religion" its flaws run the gamut from the serious to the silly. In the category of serious, the *Book of Mormon* contains modalistic language that militates against the biblical doctrine of the Trinity (Ether 3:14). In the category of silly, a man struggles to catch his breath after having his head cut off (Ether 15:31).

Furthermore, while archeology is a powerful testimony to the accuracy of the Bible the same cannot be said for the *Book of Mormon*. Not only is there no archeological evidence for a language such as "reformed Egyptian hieroglyphics," there is no archeological support for lands such as the "land of Moron" (Ether 7:6). Nor is there any archeological evidence to buttress the notion that the Jaredites, Nephites, and Lamanites migrated from Israel to the Americas. On the contrary, both archeology and anthropology demonstrate conclusively that the people and places chronicled in the *Book of Mormon* are little more than the product of a fertile imagination.

Finally, Joseph Smith asserted that the golden plates were translated "by the power of God" and produced "the most correct of any book on earth." Joseph F. Smith, the sixth president of the Mormon church, went so far as to say that the words were not only correct but "every letter was given to [Smith] by the gift and power of God." In reality however, the *Book of Mormon* has had to be corrected thousands of times to compensate for Smith's poor grammar and spelling. The *Book of Mormon* is fraught with other errors as well. For example, "Benjamin" was changed to "Mosiah" when Mormon leaders realized that in the chronology of the *Book of Mormon* King

*How millions can take
the Book of Mormon seriously is almost
beyond comprehension.*

Benjamin had already died—thus he would have been hard pressed to "interpret" the engravings mentioned in Mosiah 21:28. Perhaps the greatest crack in the credibility of the *Book of Mormon* is that whole sections were derived directly from the King James Version of the Bible—this despite the fact that according to Mormon chronology, the *Book of Mormon* predates the King James Version by more than a thousand years.

Little wonder that Mormons accept the *Book of Mormon* based on a "burning in the bosom" rather than on history and evidence.

For further study, see Jerald and Sandra Tanner, *The Changing World of Mormonism* (Chicago: Moody Press, 1980).

GALATIANS 1:6–9

"I am astonished that you are so quickly deserting the one who called you by the grace of Christ and are turning to a different gospel—which is really no gospel at all. Evidently some people are throwing you into confusion and are trying to pervert the gospel of Christ. But even if we or an angel from heaven should preach a gospel other than the one we preached to you, let him be eternally condemned! As we have already said, so now I say again: If anybody is preaching to you a gospel other than what you accepted, let him be eternally condemned!"

What Sets Christianity Apart from an Eastern Worldview?

hile it has become increasingly popular to merge Eastern spirituality with biblical Christianity, the chasm that separates these worldviews is an unbridgeable gulf.

First, in an Eastern worldview God is an impersonal force or principle. In sharp distinction, the God of Christianity is a personal being who manifests such communicable attributes as spirituality, rationality, and morality (John 4:24; Colossians 3:10; Ephesians 4:24).

Furthermore, in an Eastern worldview humanity's goal is to become one with nature because nature is God. In this sense, the Eastern worldview is pantheistic—in other words, "God is all and all is God." Conversely, Christianity teaches that man is created in the image and likeness of his Creator and as such is distinct from both nature and God (Genesis 1:26–27).

Finally, in an Eastern worldview truth is realized through intuition rather than through the cognitive thinking process. In contrast, Christianity teaches that truth is realized through revelation (Hebrews 1:1–2), which is apprehended by the intellect (Luke 1:1–4), and then embraced by the heart (Mark 12:29–31).

For further study, see James W. Sire, *The Universe Next Door: A Basic Worldview Catalog*, third ed. (Downers Grove, Ill.: InterVarsity Press, 1997); Charles Strohmer, *The Gospel and the New Spirituality* (Nashville: Thomas Nelson, 1996).

ROMANS 1:25
*"They exchanged the truth of God for a lie,
and worshiped and
served created things rather than the Creator."*

CAN REINCARNATION
AND RESURRECTION BE RECONCILED?

A n ever-growing number of people in both the church and the culture have come to believe that reincarnation and resurrection can be reconciled. In fact, multitudes have embraced the odd predilection that Scripture actually promotes reincarnation. In reality, however, the Bible makes it crystal clear that reincarnation and resurrection are mutually exclusive.

To begin with, the resurrectionist view of *one death* per person is mutually exclusive from the reincarnationist view of an on-going cycle of death and rebirth. The writer of Hebrews emphatically states that human beings are "destined to die *once*, and after that to face judgment" (Hebrews 9:27). In sharp contrast to a worldview in which humanity perfects itself through an endless cycle of birth and rebirth, the Christian worldview maintains that we are vicariously perfected by the righteousness of Christ (Philippians 3:9).

Furthermore, the biblical teaching of *one body* per person demonstrates that the gulf between reincarnation and resurrection can never be bridged. Rather than the *transmigration* of our souls into different bodies, the apostle Paul explains that Christ "will *transform* our lowly bodies" (Philippians 3:21). He explicitly says that the body that dies is the very body that rises (1 Corinthians 15:42–44).

Finally, the Christian belief that there is only *one way* to God categorically demonstrates that resurrection and reincarnation can never be reconciled. As Christ himself put it, "I am *the* way and *the* truth and *the* life. No one comes to the Father except through me" (John 14:6). If Christ is truly God, his claim to be the only way has to be taken seriously. If, on the other hand, he is merely one more person in a pantheon of pretenders, his proclamations can be pushed aside easily. That is precisely why the resurrection is axiomatic to Christianity. Through his resurrection Christ demonstrated that he does not stand in a line of peers with Buddha, Baha'u'llah, Krishna, or any other founder of a world religion. They died and are *still* dead, but Christ is risen.

Ultimately, resurrection and reincarnation can never be reconciled because the former is a historical fact while the latter is but a Hindu fantasy.

*Resurrection and
reincarnation can never be
reconciled because
the former is a historical fact
while the latter is
but a Hindu fantasy.*

For further study, see Hank Hanegraaff, *Resurrection* (Nashville: Word Publishing, 2000), Chapter 14.

Hebrews 9:27-28

"Just as man is destined to die once, and after that to face judgment, so Christ was sacrificed once to take away the sins of many people; and he will appear a second time, not to bear sin, but to bring salvation to those who are waiting for him."

WHAT IS THE NEW AGE MOVEMENT?

ot everyone who wears a cross is a
Christian. Likewise, not everyone who
owns a crystal is a New Ager. To accurately
identify New Agers we must move beyond superficial
symbols such as crystals, unicorns, and rainbows to
identify their beliefs and practices.

First, New Agers hold to pantheistic monism.
Thus, in their view, God is all, all is God, and all is
one. Additionally, they believe that the universe
operates under the law of karma and its corollary,
the doctrine of reincarnation.

Furthermore, the goal of New Agers is to
spiritually evolve and tap into their human potential
through the help of "ascended masters" or spirit
guides. To attain such enlightenment New Agers
engage in occult practices such as astrology, magic,
psychic healing, out-of-body experiences, and
meditation. In New Age meditation, for example,
the goal is to stamp out the self—and to become
one with the impersonal cosmic consciousness of
the universe. In sharp contrast, biblical meditation

seeks to center one's self on the personal Creator of the universe—and does so through a singular focus on Scripture (Joshua 1:8).

Finally, New Agers share the vision of a coming "age of Aquarius" that is marked by global peace, prosperity, and planetary transformation. Their ultimate goal is encapsulated in such catch phrases as "global village" and "planetary consciousness." Far from being a monolith, however, the New Age movement is a multifaceted amorphous network of organizations such as *Planetary Initiative for the World*, *Divine Light Mission*, and *Self Realization Fellowship*, loosely linked yet autonomous.

For further study, see Douglas R. Groothuis, *Unmasking the New Age* (Downers Grove, Ill.: InterVarsity Press, 1986); for a comprehensive work, see Elliot Miller, *A Crash Course on The New Age Movement* (Grand Rapids: Baker Book House, 1989).

DEUTERONOMY 18:9–13

"When you enter the land the LORD your God is giving you, do not learn to imitate the detestable ways of the nations there. Let no one be found among you who sacrifices his son or daughter in the fire, who practices divination or sorcery, interprets omens, engages in witchcraft, or casts spells, or who is a medium or spiritist or who consults the dead. Anyone who does these things is detestable to the LORD."

WHAT IS WRONG WITH ASTROLOGY?

s Charles Strohmer has well said, "astrology has been debunked more than the tooth fairy and cheered more than the Pope." Despite the fact that it is denounced by Scripture, debunked by science, and is demonstrably superstitious, humankind's fascination with astrology continues unabated. While multitudes view astrology as a harmless pastime, in reality it is a rigged "game" replete with self-validating prophecies and a dangerous form of divination.

First, Scripture clearly condemns astrology as a practice that is "detestable to the Lord" (Deuteronomy 18:10–12). Isaiah goes so far as to say that the counsel of the "astrologers" and "stargazers who make predictions month by month" not only wore out the Babylonians but could not save them from their future ruin (Isaiah 47:13–14). Despite the clear condemnation of Scripture, there are those who maintain that there is a biblical precedent for using stars to chart the future. As a case in point, they cite the star guiding the Magi to the Messiah. However,

*While multitudes view
astrology as a harmless pastime,
in reality it is a rigged "game" replete
with self-validating prophecies and a
dangerous form of divination.*

a quick look at context reveals that this star was not used to *foretell* the future but to *forth tell* the future. In other words, the star of Bethlehem did not *prophesy* the birth of Christ; it *pronounced* the birth of Christ (Matthew 2:9–10).

Furthermore, science has debunked astrology as a pseudoscience based on the odd predilection that *galaxies* rather than *genes* determine inherited human characteristics. Not only so, astrology cannot account for the problem posed by mass tragedies and twins. People with a wide variety of horoscopes all perished on 9/11/2001. And twins born under the same sign of the zodiac frequently end up with widely diverse futures. Even King Nebuchadnezzar's astrologers recognized the impotence of their craft. When Nebuchadnezzar asked them to remind him of his dream and then interpret it, they responded in terror, saying, "no man on earth can do what the king asks!" (Daniel 2:10)

Finally, astrology subverts the natural use of the stars, which God ordains, for a superstitious use, which He disdains. Genesis 1:14 points to the natural use of the stars to separate the day from the night, to serve as signs that mark seasons, days, and years, and to illuminate the earth. They also can rightly be used for varied purposes ranging from navigation to natural revelation. Thus, sailors may use astronavigation to chart their course; however, saints may not use astrology to chart their careers.

For further study, see Charles R. Strohmer, *America's Fascination with Astrology: Is it Healthy?* (Greenville, South Carolina: Emerald House, 1998).

ISAIAH 47:13–14

"Let your astrologers come forward, those stargazers
who make predictions month by month,
let them save you from what is coming upon you.
Surely, they are like stubble; the fire will burn them
up. They cannot even save themselves from the power
of the flame . . . Each of them goes on in his error;
there is not one that can save you."

Can We Be Certain
that Evolution Is a Myth?

r. Louis Bounoure, former director of research at the French National Center for Scientific Research, calls evolution "a fairy tale for grown-ups." I call it a cruel hoax! In fact, the arguments that support evolutionary theory are astonishingly weak.

First, the fossil record is an embarrassment to evolutionists. No verifiable transitions from one kind to another have as yet been found. Charles Darwin had an excuse; in his day fossil finds were relatively scarce. Today, however, we have an abundance of fossils. Still, we have yet to find even one legitimate transition from one kind to another.

Furthermore, in Darwin's day such enormously complex structures as a human egg were thought to be quite simple—for all practical purposes, little more than a microscopic blob of gelatin. Today, we know that a fertilized human egg is among the most organized, complex structures in the universe. In an age of scientific enlightenment, it is incredible to think people are willing to maintain that something so vastly complex arose by chance. Like an egg or the human eye, the universe is a masterpiece of precision and design that could not have come into existence by chance.

In an age of scientific enlightenment,
it is incredible to think people are willing to maintain that
something so vastly complex arose by chance.

Finally, while chance is a blow to the theory of evolution, the laws of science are a bullet to its head. The basic laws of science, including the laws of *effects* and their causes—*energy conservation* and *entropy*—undergird the creation model for origins and undermine the evolutionary hypothesis. While I would fight for a person's right to have faith in science fiction, we must resist evolutionists who attempt to brainwash people into thinking that evolution is science.

For further study, see Hank Hanegraaff, *Fatal Flaws: What Evolutionists Don't Want You To Know* (Nashville: W Publishing, 2003); Phillip E. Johnson, *Darwin on Trial*, second edition (Downers Grove, Ill.: InterVarsity Press, 1993).

"The heavens declare the glory of God;
the skies proclaim the work of his hands.
Day after day they pour forth speech;
night after night they display knowledge.
There is no speech or language
where their voice is not heard.
Their voice goes out into all the earth,
their words to the ends of the world."

Is Archaeopteryx the Missing Link
between Dinosaurs and Birds?

W henever I say that there are no transitions from one species to another, someone inevitably brings up *Archaeopteryx*. This happens so frequently that I've decided to coin a word for the experience: *pseudosaur*. *Pseudo* means false and *saur* refers to a dinosaur or a reptile (literally lizard). Thus, a pseudosaur is a false link between reptiles (such as dinosaurs) and birds. Myriad evidences demonstrate conclusively that *Archaeopteryx* is a full-fledged bird; not a missing link.

First, fossils of both *Archaeopteryx* and the kinds of dinosaurs *Archaeopteryx* supposedly descended from have been found in a fine-grained German limestone formation said to be Late Jurassic (the Jurassic period is said to have begun 190 million years ago, lasting 54 million years). Thus, *Archaeopteryx* is not a likely candidate as the missing link, since birds and their alleged ancestral dinosaurs thrived during the same period.

Furthermore, initial *Archaeopteryx* fossil finds gave no evidence of a bony sternum, which led paleontologists to conclude that *Archaeopteryx* could not fly or was a poor flyer. However, in April 1993 a seventh specimen was reported that included a bony sternum. Thus, there is no further doubt that *Archaeopteryx* was as suited for power flying as any modern bird.

Finally, to say that *Archaeopteryx* is a missing link between reptiles and birds, one must believe that scales evolved into feathers for flight. Air friction acting on genetic mutation supposedly frayed the outer edges of reptilian scales. Thus, in the course of millions of years, scales became increasingly like feathers until, one day, the perfect feather emerged. To say the least, this idea must stretch the credulity of even the most ardent evolutionists.

These and myriad other factors overwhelmingly exclude *Archaeopteryx* as a missing link between birds and dinosaurs. The sober fact is that *Archaeopteryx* appears abruptly in the fossil record, with masterfully engineered wings and feathers common in the birds observable today. Even the late Stephen Jay Gould of Harvard and Niles Eldridge of the American Museum of Natural History, both militant evolutionists, have concluded that *Archaeopteryx* cannot be viewed as a transitional form.

For further study, see Duane T. Gish, Evolution: *The Fossils Still Say No!* (El Cajon, Calif.: Institute for Creation Research, 1995); and Jonathan Wells, *Icons of Evolution: Science or Myth?* (Washington D.C.: Regnery, 2000).

GENESIS 1:25

"God made the wild animals according to their kinds, the livestock according to their kinds, and all the creatures that move along the ground according to their kinds. And God saw that it was good."

IS EVOLUTIONISM RACIST?

irst, while not all evolutionists are racists, the theory of evolution is racist in the extreme. In his book *The Descent of Man* Charles Darwin speculated, "At some future period, not very distant as measured by centuries, the civilized races of man will almost certainly exterminate, and replace, the savage races throughout the world." In addition, he subtitled his magnum opus *The Preservation of Favored Races in the Struggle for Life.* Thomas Huxley, who coined the term *agnostic* and was the man most responsible for advancing Darwinian doctrine, went so far as to say, "No rational man cognizant of the facts, believes that the average Negro is the equal, still less the superior, of the white man." Huxley was not only militantly racist but also lectured frequently against the resurrection of Jesus Christ in whom "[we] are all one" (Galatians 3:28).

Furthermore, for evolution to succeed, it is as crucial that the unfit die as that the fittest survive. Marvin Lubenow graphically portrays the ghastly

The worldview of Hitler
was completely consistent with the
teachings of Darwin.

consequences of such beliefs in his book *Bones of Contention*: "If the unfit survived indefinitely, they would continue to 'infect' the fit with their less fit genes. The result is that the more fit genes would be diluted and compromised by the less fit genes, and evolution could not take place." Adolf Hitler's philosophy that Jews were subhuman and that Aryans were supermen led to the extermination of six million Jews. In the words of Sir Arthur Keith, a militant anti-Christian physical anthropologist: "The German Fuhrer, as I have consistently maintained, is an evolutionist; he has consistently sought to make the practices of Germany conform to the theory of evolution." It is significant to note that crusaders who used force to further their creeds in the name of God were acting in direct opposition to the teachings of Christ, while the worldview of Hitler, however, was completely consistent with the teachings of Darwin. Indeed, social Darwinism has provided the scientific substructure for some of the most significant atrocities in human history.

Finally, while the evolutionary racism of Darwin's day is politically incorrect today, current biology textbooks still promote vestiges of racism. For example, the inherently racist recapitulation theory* is not only common fare in science curricula but has been championed in our generation by such luminaries as Carl Sagan. This despite the fact that modern studies in molecular genetics have demonstrated the utter falsity of the recapitulation theory. The fact that recapitulation is inherently racist is underscored by no less an evolutionary authority than Stephen Jay Gould who lamented that "recapitulation provided a convenient focus for the pervasive racism of white scientists" in the modern era.

For further study, see Hank Hanegraaff, *Fatal Flaws: What Evolutionists Don't Want You to Know* (Nashville: W Publishing, 2003).

GENESIS 1:27
"God created man in his own image,
in the image of God he created them; male and
female he created them."

*Recapitulation theory, better known by the popular evolutionary phrase, "Ontogeny recapitulates phylogeny," is the odd predilection that in the course of an embryo's development the embryo repeats or recapitulates the evolutionary history of its species.

Under the banner of "theistic evolution," a growing number of Christians maintain that God used evolution as His method for creation. This, in my estimation, is the worst of all possibilities. It is one thing to believe in evolution; it is quite another to blame God for it. Not only is *theistic evolution* a contradiction in terms—like the phrase *flaming snowflakes*—but in the words of the Nobel prize winning evolutionist Jacques Monod:

"[Natural] selection is the blindest, and most cruel way of evolving new species. . . . The struggle for life and elimination of the weakest is a horrible process, against which our whole modern ethic revolts. . . . I am surprised that a Christian would defend the idea that this is the process which God more or less set up in order to have evolution."

First, the biblical account of creation specifically states that God created living creatures according to their own "kinds" (Genesis 1:24–25). As confirmed by science, the DNA for a fetus is not the DNA for a frog, and the DNA for a frog is not the DNA for a fish. Rather the DNA of a fetus, frog, or fish is uniquely programmed for reproduction after its own kind. Thus while the Bible allows for *micro*evolution (transitions within "the kinds") it does not allow for *macro*evolution (amoebas evolving into apes or apes evolving into astronauts).

Furthermore, evolutionary biology cannot account for metaphysical realities such as ego and ethos. Without data demonstrating that physical processes can produce metaphysical realities, there is no warrant for dogmatically declaring that humans evolved from hominids.

Finally, an omnipotent, omniscient God does not have to painfully plod through millions of mistakes, misfits, and mutations in order to have fellowship with humans. As the biblical account of creation confirms he can create humans instantaneously (Genesis 2:7).

Evolutionism is fighting for its very life. Rather than prop it up with theories like theistic evolution, thinking people everywhere must be on the vanguard of demonstrating its demise.

For further study, see J. P. Moreland and John Mark Reynolds, eds., *Three Views on Creation and Evolution* (Grand Rapids: Zondervan Publishing House, 1999).

"'The God who made the world and everything in it is the Lord of heaven and earth and does not live in temples built by hands. And he is not served by human hands, as if he needed anything, because he himself gives all men life and breath and everything else. From one man he made every nation of men, that they should inhabit the whole earth; and he determined the times set for them and the exact places where they should live. God did this so that men would seek him and perhaps reach out for him and find him, though he is not far from each one of us.'"

DID DARWIN HAVE
A DEATHBED CONVERSION?

In order to demonstrate the falsity of evolution, Bible-believing Christians for more than a century have passed on the story of Charles Darwin's deathbed conversion. Evolutionists have attempted to counter them by loudly protesting that Darwin died believing that Christianity was a fraud and that chance was the creator.

In response, it should first be noted that whether Darwin did or did not renounce evolution does *not* speak to the issue of whether or not evolution is true or false. Maybe Darwin renounced evolution because he was senile or he had taken a mind-altering drug. He may have even just hedged his bets with some "eternal fire insurance."

Furthermore, as followers of the One who proclaimed himself to be not only "the way" and "the life" but also "the truth" (John 14:6) we must set the standard for the evolutionist, *not* vice versa. James Fegan was correct in calling the Darwin legend "an

There is no substantial evidence
that Darwin ever repented.

illustration of the recklessness with which the Protestant Controversialists seek to support any cause they are advocating."

Finally, in *The Darwin Legend*, James Moore painstakingly documents the fact that there is *no* substantial evidence that Darwin ever repented, but there is abundant evidence that he consistently held to his evolutionary paradigm.

For further study, see James Moore, *The Darwin Legend* (Grand Rapids: Baker Books, 1994).

EXODUS 20:16
*"You shall not give
false testimony against your neighbor."*

How Can a Person
Find More Bible Answers?

he Bible Answer Book addresses some of the most significant questions I've been asked during fifteen years of hosting the *Bible Answer Man* radio broadcast. In well over three thousand *live* broadcasts I've answered thousands more. I invite you to ask me *your* questions live on the *Bible Answer Man* broadcast by dialing toll-free 1.888.ASK.HANK, Monday through Friday, 2:50 to 4:00 P.M., Pacific Time, or access additional answers online at www.equip.org.

Furthermore, it is your responsibility to search the Scriptures daily. My opinion is no better than anyone else's opinion unless it squares with Scripture. The Apostle Paul commended the Berean believers "for they received the message with great eagerness *and examined the Scriptures every day to see if what Paul said was true*" (Acts 17:11, emphasis added).

Finally, it is crucial that you get into the Word of God and get the Word of God into you. If you fail to eat well-balanced meals on a regular basis, you eventually will suffer the physical consequences. Likewise, if you do not regularly feed on the Word of God, you will suffer spiritual consequences. Jesus said, "Man does not live on bread alone, but on every word that comes from the mouth of God" (Matthew 4:4). Great physical meals are one thing; great spiritual M-E-A-L-S are quite another:

Memorize: As a result of teaching memory seminars for over twenty years I am convinced that anyone, regardless of age or acumen, can memorize Scripture. God has called you to write his Word on the tablet of your heart (Proverbs 7:1–3; Deuteronomy 6:6), and with the call he has provided the ability. Your mind is like a muscle. If you exercise it, you will increase its capacity to remember and recall information. If you do not, like a muscle, it will atrophy. A good place to start memorizing is Joshua 1:8: "Do not let this Book of the Law depart from your mouth; meditate on it day and night, so that you may be careful to do everything written in it. Then you will be prosperous and successful."

Examine: As mentioned above, the Berean believers daily examined the Scriptures to see if what Paul taught was true. For that they were commended as being noble in character. Ultimate authority was not placed in the revelation of men but in the revelation of God. The apostle Paul urged Christians to test all things (1 Thessalonians 5:21) and to be transformed by the renewing of their minds in order to discern the will of God (Romans 12:2). Examining the Scriptures requires discipline, but the dividends are dramatic.

Apply: As wonderful and worthwhile as it is to memorize and examine Scripture, it is not enough! You must take the knowledge you have gleaned from the Word of God and *apply* it in your daily life—*wisdom is the application of knowledge.* As the Master put it: "Everyone who hears these words of mine and puts them into practice is like a wise man who built his house on the rock. The rain came down, the streams rose, and the winds blew and beat against that house; yet it did not fall, because it had its foundation on the rock. But everyone who hears these words of mine and does not put them into practice is like a foolish man who built his house on sand. The rain came down, the streams rose, and the winds blew and beat against that house, and it fell with a great crash" (Matthew 7:24–27). James the brother of Jesus used irony to drive home the same point. In essence, he said that anyone who hears the Word and does not apply it is like a man who looks in a mirror and sees that his face is dirty, but doesn't wash it (James 1:23–24).

Listen: In order to apply God's directions to life experiences, you must first *listen* carefully as God speaks to you through the mystery of His Word. Like Samuel, you should say, "Speak, [Lord,] for your servant is *listening*" (1 Samuel 3:10). One of the most amazing aspects of Scripture is that it is alive and active, not dead and dull. Indeed, God still speaks today through the mystery of His Word. The Holy Spirit illumines our minds so that we may understand what he has freely given us (1 Corinthians 2:12). As Jesus so beautifully put it, "My sheep *listen* to my voice; I know them, and they follow me" (John 10:27).

Study: In *examining* Scripture, it is typically best to stick with one good Bible translation. This not only provides consistency but facilitates the process of Scripture memorization. In *studying*, however, it is helpful to use a number of good translations. To further your study of Scripture, it is necessary to have access to study tools. The toolbox of serious Scripture students should include a concordance, a commentary, and a Bible dictionary. You also might consider obtaining some of the resources suggested in *The Bible Answer Book*.

Jesus said, "I am the bread of life. He who comes to me will never go hungry, and he who believes in me will never be thirsty" (John 6:35). May the acronym M-E-A-L-S daily remind you to nourish yourself by partaking of the Bread of life.

Memorize

Examine

Apply

Listen

Study

NOTES
& MY BIBLE QUESTIONS

NOTES
& My Bible Questions

ACKNOWLEDGEMENTS

To begin with, I am deeply grateful for the gentle—sometimes not so gentle—persuasion applied by my friends Jack and Marsha Countryman—without it this volume would likely have remained an unfinished monument. My entire family treasures their friendship and faithfulness. Moreover, I am indebted to the entire J. Countryman team for producing a fabulous product. In particular, I appreciate the editorial input of Kathy Baker—you are one smart lady!

Furthermore, I would like to express appreciation for my staff, including Paul Young, Stephen Ross, and Sam Wall. So many of us have worked together for such a long time that it would be easy to take one another for granted—I cherish the fact that we do not.

Finally, I would like to acknowledge my wife, Kathy, and our kids and grandkids—Michelle, Katie, David, John Mark, Hank Jr., Christina, Paul Stephen, Faith, Grace, Lucy, Elise, and Micah—who bless me beyond measure. Above all, I am supremely thankful to my Master—because he lives I can face tomorrow.

Some of the material
in the *Bible Answer Book* has been adapted
from the author's
previously published books.

From W Publishing Group:
The FACE
The Covering
The Prayer of Jesus
The Third Day
Counterfeit Revival
Resurrection
Fatal Flaws

From Harvest House Publishers
Christianity in Crisis

ADDITIONAL RESOURCES

The following resources are recommended for further study of the topics in *The Bible Answer Book*:

Richard Abanes, *One Nation Under Gods* (New York: Four Walls Eight Windows, 2003).

Randy Alcorn, *Money, Possessions and Eternity*, rev. ed. (Wheaton, Ill.: Tyndale House Publishers, 2003).

Gleason L. Archer, *New International Encyclopedia of Bible Difficulties* (Grand Rapids: Zondervan, 1982), 79–80.

D.A. Carson, ed., *From Sabbath to Lord's Day: A Biblical, Historical, and Theological Investigation* (Eugene, Oregon: Wipf and Stock Publishers, 1999, originally published by Zondervan, 1982)

Francis J. Beckwith, *Politically Correct Death: Answering the Arguments for Abortion Rights*, (Grand Rapids: Baker Books, 1993).

The Center for Bioethics and Human Dignity —www.cbhd.org—2065 Half Day Road, Bannockburn, IL 60015 USA, Voice: 847.317.8180

J. Daryl Charles, "Sentiments as Social Justice: The Ethics of Capital Punishment," *Christian Research Journal,* Spring/Summer 1994.

Paul Copan, *That's Just Your Interpretation: Responding to Skeptics Who Challenge Your Faith* (Grand Rapids: Baker Books, 2001), 171–178.

William Lane Craig, *Reasonable Faith* (Crossway Books, 1994).

Joe Dallas, *Desires in Conflict,* updated edition (Eugene, Ore.: Harvest House Publishers, 2003).

Joe Dallas, *A Strong Delusion: Confronting the "Gay Christian" Movement* (Eugene, Ore.: Harvest House Publishers, 1996).

Millard J. Erickson, *The Word Became Flesh: A Contemporary Incarnational Christology* (Grand Rapids: Baker Book House, 1996).

Timothy George, *Is the Father of Jesus the God of Muhammad?* (Grand Rapids: Zondervan, 2002).

R. Douglas Geivett and Gary R. Habermas, eds., *In Defense of Miracles: A Comprehensive Case for God's Action in History* (Downers Grove, Ill.: InterVarsity Press, 1997).

Norman L. Geisler & Abdul Saleeb, *Answering Islam* (Grand Rapids: Baker Books, 2002).

Norman L. Geisler, *Christian Ethics: Options and Issues* (Grand Rapids: Baker Book House, 1989), chapter 7.

Norman L. Geisler, *Baker Encyclopedia of Christian Apologetics* (Grand Rapids: Baker Books, 1999), 553–554; see also 283–288.

Norman L. Geisler and Douglas E. Potter, "From Ashes to Ashes: Is Burial the Only Christian Option?" *Christian Research Journal*, summer 1998, available at www.equip.org/free/dc765.htm.

Norman L. Geisler and Ralph E. MacKenzie, *Roman Catholics and Evangelicals: Agreements and Differences* (Grand Rapids: Baker Books, 1995).

Duane T. Gish, *Evolution: the Fossils Still Say No!* (El Cajon, Calif.: Institute for Creation Research, 1995).

Douglas R. Groothuis, *Unmasking the New Age* (Downers Grove, Ill.: InterVarsity Press, 1986).

Os Guinness, *Time for Truth* (Grand Rapids: Baker Books, 2000).

Gary R. Habermas and J. P. Moreland, *Beyond Death: Exploring the Evidence for Immortality* (Wheaton, Ill.: Crossway Books, 1998).

Hank Hanegraaff, *Christianity in Crisis* (Eugene, Ore.: Harvest House Publishers, 1993), Part 2.

Hank Hanegraaff, *Counterfeit Revival: Looking for God in All the Wrong Places*, rev. ed. (Nashville: Word Publishing, 2001).

Hank Hanegraaff, *The Covering: God's Plan to Protect You from Evil* (Nashville: W Publishing Group, 2002).

Hank Hanegraaff, "Does your relationship with God make you sure you will go to heaven when you die?" pamphlet, available through Christian Research Institute, P.O. Box 7000, Rancho Santa Margarita, California 92688; 1–888–7000–CRI; www.equip.org.

Hank Hanegraaff, *The F.A.C.E. That Demonstrates the Farce of Evolution* (Nashville: Word Publishing, 1998).

Hank Hanegraaff, *Fatal Flaws: What Evolutionists Don't Want You To Know* (Nashville: W Publishing, 2003).

Hank Hanegraaff, "How to Find a Healthy Church" (Rancho Santa Margarita, Calif.: Christian Research Institute, 2003), pamphlet.

Hank Hanegraaff, "The Indwelling of the Holy Spirit," *Christian Research Journal*, Spring 1997, available at http://www.equip.org/free/DS575.pdf.

Hank Hanegraaff "Karla Faye Tucker and Capital Punishment," CRI Perspective CP1304, Christian Research Institute, P O Box 7000, Rancho Santa Margarita, Calif., 92688; 1–888–7000–CRI.

Hank Hanegraaff, *The Prayer of Jesus: Secrets to Real Intimacy with God* (Nashville: W Publishing Group, 2001).

"Questions and Answers: Genesis 6:4," available from Christian Research Institute, P O Box 7000, Rancho Santa Margarita, California 92688, or call 1–888–7000–CRI

Hank Hanegraaff, *Resurrection* (Nashville: Word Publishing, 2000).

Hank Hanegraaff, "Safe and Secure" (Rancho Santa Margarita, Calif.: Christian Research Institute, 1996).

Hank Hanegraaff, *The Third Day* (Nashville: W Publishing Group, 2003).

Hank Hanegraaff, "The Unforgivable Sin," available from Christian Research Institute at http://www.equip.org/free/DU250.htm.

Hank Hanegraaff, "What about Halloween?" (Rancho Santa Margarita: Christian Research Institute, 2001), pamphlet.

Carl F. H. Henry, *Basic Christian Doctrines,* (Grand Rapids: Baker Book House, 1962).

Phillip E. Johnson, *Darwin on Trial,* second edition (Downers Grove, Ill.: InterVarsity Press, 1993).

Peter J. Kreeft, *Everything You Ever Wanted to Know About Heaven, but Never Dreamed of Asking* (San Francisco: Ignatius Press, 1990).

C.S. Lewis, *Mere Christianity* (New York: Macmillan, 1952).

C.S. Lewis, *The Screwtape Letters* (New York: Macmillan, 1982).

Gordon R. Lewis, "Attributes of God," in Walter A. Elwell, ed., *Evangelical Dictionary of Theology,* 2nd edition (Grand Rapids: Baker Academic, 2001), 492–499.

John MacArthur, *Hard to Believe: The High Cost and Infinite Value of Following Jesus* (Nashville: Thomas Nelson Publishers, 2003).

John MacArthur, *Why One Way? Defending an Exclusive Claim in an Inclusive World* (Nashville: W Publishing Group, 2002).

Paul Maier, *The First Christmas* (Grand Rapids: Kregel Publications, 2001).

Elliot Miller, *A Crash Course on The New Age Movement* (Grand Rapids: Baker Book House, 1989).

Bruce Milne, *Know the Truth* (Downer's Grove: Intervarsity Press: 1998), pages 189–191.

James Moore, *The Darwin Legend* (Grand Rapids: Baker Books, 1994).

J. P. Moreland and John Mark Reynolds, eds., *Three Views on Creation and Evolution* (Grand Rapids: ZondervanPublishingHouse, 1999).

Ronald H. Nash, *The Gospel and the Greeks* (Richardson, Texas: Probe Books, 1992).

Ronald Nash, *Is Jesus the Only Savior?* (Grand Rapids: Zondervan, 1994).

J. I. Packer, *Knowing God* (Downers Grove, Ill.: InterVarsity Press, 1993).

Robert A. Peterson, *Hell on Trial: The Case for Eternal Punishment* (Phillipsburg, New Jersey: Presbyterian and Reformed Press, 1995).

John Piper, *Desiring God: Meditations of a Christian Hedonist* (Sisters, Ore.: Multnomah Publishers, 1986), chapter 7.

David A. Reed, *Answering Jehovah's Witnesses: Subject by Subject* (Grand Rapids: Baker Book House, 1996).

Ron Rhodes, *The Challenge of the Cults and New Religions* (Grand Rapids: Zondervan, 2001).

Ron Rhodes, *Reasoning from the Scriptures with the Jehovah's Witnesses* (Eugene, Ore.: Harvest House Publishers, 1993).

James W. Sire, *The Universe Next Door: A Basic Worldview Catalog*, third ed. (Downers Grove, Ill.: InterVarsity Press, 1997).

R.C. Sproul, *Not A Chance: The Myth of Chance in Modern Science and Cosmology* (Grand Rapids: Baker Book House, 1994).

R. C. Sproul, *Reason to Believe* (Grand Rapids: Zondervan, 1982).

Lee Strobel, *The Case for Christ* (Grand Rapids: Zondervan, 1998).

Lee Strobel, *The Case for Faith* (Grand Rapids: Zondervan, 2000).

Charles R. Strohmer, *America's Fascination with Astrology: Is it Healthy?* (Greenville, South Carolina: Emerald House, 1998).

Charles Strohmer, *The Gospel and the New Spirituality* (Nashville: Thomas Nelson, 1996).

Joni Eareckson Tada and Steven Estes, *When God Weeps* (Grand Rapids: Zondervan, 1997).

Jerald and Sandra Tanner, *The Changing World of Mormonism* (Chicago: Moody, 1980).

Peter Toon, *The Ascension of our Lord* (Nashville: Thomas Nelson, 1984)

Jonathan Wells, *Icons of Evolution: Science or Myth?* (Washington D.C.: Regnery, 2000).

James R. White, *The Forgotten Trinity* (Minneapolis: Bethany House, 2001).

CHRISTIAN RESEARCH INSTITUTE

The Christian Research Institute (CRI) exists to provide Christians worldwide with carefully researched information and well-reasoned answers that encourage them in their faith and equip them to intelligently represent it to people influenced by ideas and teachings that assault or undermine orthodox, biblical Christianity. In carrying out this mission, CRI's strategy is expressed by the acronym *E-Q-U-I-P*:

The "E" in EQUIP represents the word *essentials*. CRI is committed to the maxim: "In essentials unity, in nonessentials liberty, and in all things charity."

The "Q" in the acronym EQUIP represents the word *questions*. In addition to focusing on essentials, CRI answers people's questions regarding cults, culture, and Christianity.

The "U" in the word EQUIP represents the word *user-friendly*. As much as possible, CRI is committed to taking complex issues and making them understandable and accessible to the lay Christian.

This brings us to the "I" in EQUIP, which stands for *integrity.* Recall Paul's admonition: "Watch your life and doctrine closely. Persevere in them, because if you do, you will save both yourself and your hearers."

Finally, the "P" in the acronym EQUIP represents the word *para-church.* CRI is deeply committed to the local church as the God-ordained vehicle for equipping, evangelism, and education.

Contact
Christian Research Institute:

By Mail:
CRI United States
P.O. Box 7000
Rancho Santa Margarita, CA 92688–2124

In Canada:
CRI Canada
56051 Airways P.O.
Calgary, Alberta T2E 8K5
For information (Canada) (403) 571–6363
By Phone:
24–hour Customer Service (U.S.) (949) 858–6100
24–hour Toll–Free Credit Card Line 1 (888) 7000–CRI
Fax (949) 858–6111
24-Hour Toll-Free Customer Service (Canada)
1 (800) 665–5851 (orders and donations only)

On the Internet:
www.equip.org

On the Broadcast:
To contact the *Bible Answer Man* broadcast with your
questions, call toll free in the U.S. and Canada, 1 (888)
ASK HANK (275–4265), Monday-Friday, 2:30 P.M. to
4:00 P.M. Pacific Time.

For a list of stations airing the *Bible Answer Man* or
to listen to the broadcast via the Internet, log onto our
Web site at www.equip.org.